Fifty Great Escapes

Wisdom With Understanding is Better Than Rubies

Lurine Karon Greenberg
Fine Arts Collection

Prestel Verlag
Königinstrasse 9, D-80539 Munich
Tel. +49 (89) 38 17 09-0
Fax +49 (89) 38 17 09-35
www.prestel.de

Prestel Publishing Ltd.
4, Bloomsbury Place, London WC1A 2QA
Tel. +44 (020) 7323-5004
Fax +44 (020) 7636-8004

Prestel Publishing
900 Broadway, Suite 603
New York, N.Y. 10003
Tel. +1 (212) 995-2720
Fax +1 (212) 995-2733
www.prestel.com

Library of Congress Control Number 2006928801.
The Deutsche Bibliothek holds a record of this publication
in the Deutsche Nationalbibliographie; detailed
bibliographical data can be found under: http://dnb.dde.
de

The euro and dollar prices in this book were correct at
the time of going to press. The Author and Publisher
cannot accept any responsibility for any loss, injury or
inconvenience resulting from the use of information
contained in this guide.

Prestel books are available worldwide. Please contact
your nearest bookseller or one of the above addresses for
information concerning your local distributor.

Editorial direction: Philippa Hurd
Picture research: Natalie Buchholz
Design, layout and typesetting: SMITH
Victoria Forrest, London
Origination: Dexter Graphics, London
Printing and binding: Print Consult, Munich

Printed in Slovakia

ISBN 3-7913-3645-2
978-3-7913-3645-9

Fifty Great Escapes

A Global Guide to Creativity
Jonathan Lee

PRESTEL

MUNICH · BERLIN · LONDON · NEW YORK

Inspiration

Creation

Big Break

Hell-raising

Reinvention

Jonathan Lee London

Welcome to a book about transformation.

Travel is so much more than an act of relocation. It can entertain and revitalise, enlighten, enrage, appal or scare you witless. It can help you forget, relive or reinvent. Travel can throw burning issues into stark relief, camouflage them behind palm fronds or smother them in a fug of cocktails. The best travel, though, reveals some kind of truth about yourself or the world. This book recounts such moments of discovery. And our guides for these journeys are some of the greatest creatives who ever lived.

This book explores how artists have been inspired by travel and their environment to create their work. I've focused on fifty examples—spanning poets, novelists, sculptors, filmmakers and musicians—and sought out an additional hundred places that could provide a transformative experience of your own. As you will discover, it's never quite as simple as "went on holiday, wrote a best-seller". Some acts of creation involved great hardship and tragedy—see for example, Aleister Crowley's disastrous mountain climb in Nepal or Paul Gauguin's disease-wracked years in Tahiti. Other candidates have been brave to the point of foolhardiness: Robert Capa tumbled onto Omaha Beach on D-Day armed with just a camera, while Banksy met loaded rifles with cans of spray paint at the Separation Barrier in the Occupied Territories. Some creative acts span years— William Walton's Mediterranean garden is still being tended by his widow, for example— while others last just a few furious minutes, as a visit to Jackson Pollock's paint-spattered Long Island barn will prove. All these works have one thing in common: a quality that reaches deep and that will endure.

This book is designed to buoy the spirits of the cultural traveller and the budding creative alike. Where can the cash-strapped live cheaply, eat well and feel inspired? Where can you detox, re-think and start afresh? How can you achieve in a world where potential backers, editors or gallery owners habitually shut doors in your face? Where are the best places on the planet to celebrate and indulge? At least some of the answers should lie within these pages.

While researching this book I have tried to get as close as possible to the artists and their experiences. This has involved a huge amount of travel—from the bustle of Jorge Luis Borges' Buenos Aires to the Beatles' Rishikesh, from Aldous Huxley's sublime Lake Atitlàn in Guatemala to Ernest Hemingway's favourite watering hole in Venice, and from Arthur Conan Doyle's English moorland to Leonardo da Vinci's Milan. Where possible I've tried to interview the artist, or someone close to them and their work. Photographer LeRoy Grannis, now in his eighties, paddled me out into the swell of the 1960s' surf boom, while avant-garde artist Christian Marclay steered me through the 1970s' punk scene of New York's East Village. Lee Miller's son, Antony Penrose, brought his mother's encounters with bears in rural Romania to life, while former seaman Maurice Watson conjured up the storm that scuppered his freighter in 1941, an event that inspired the Ealing comedy, Whisky Galore!. It's been a privilege to hear about such experiences first hand.

I've tried to dispel a few myths about the creative process too. Many of us think we can become great writers by holing up in a mountain cabin and staring at a blank sheet of paper, awaiting inspiration. But as this book attempts to show, the process is far more complex and challenging. Even Leonardo da Vinci had to massage his CV to secure patronage from the Duke of Milan, while Mozart spent several uncomfortable months rattling through the Italian countryside by horse and carriage to publicise his prodigious talents. Many, such as Jerome K. Jerome, only enjoyed financial security after several years of low-paid work, while many successful artists never managed to give up "the day job" at all.

You will find that this book abounds with connections, the crossing of paths and coincidences. Lee Miller, Picasso and Robert Capa were all acquainted. Arthur Conan Doyle and Joseph Conrad both wrote works to raise awareness about the crisis in the Congo. The sculptor, Antony Gormley, whose figures can be found striding across a salt pan in Western Australia, also joined a Cape Farewell expedition to the High Artic. Meanwhile Tangier, Soho, New York's East Village, Monte Verità and Paris' Café de Flore have attracted communities of writers, painters and poets for much of the 20th century.

Although I've focused on art in the broadest sense, this is also a book for people who never have, nor ever intend, to pick up a paintbrush, pen a poem, make a film or construct a radical piece of installation art. These emotional journeys are familiar to all of us: the trials of ambition, ego, success, tragedy and failure are universal. I've marshalled the stories into five chapters—inspiration, creation, big break, hell-raising and reinvention—because most of us, artists or not, seek such experiences throughout our lives.

I set out to write a cultural "travel-guide-meets-inspirational-manual", a book that captures the drama of human endeavour while touching upon pressing global issues such as climate change, capitalism, space travel, child poverty, colonial exploitation and war. It's been a challenging and intense process, but I've also tried to incorporate humour too. There can be few books that take you from Butlins to the West Bank and from a Prada store in the Texan desert to the planet Mars. I hope you enjoy the ride.

HOW TO GET THERE

The nearest major airport is in the capital, Guatemala City, around 150 km and some four hours' drive away. Good bus services link all Guatemala's main cities and towns, and you'll probably be dropped off at the lake's main tourist hub, Panajachel. From there take a boat to your village of choice. Bear in mind that some villages have a distinct following —some drawing fans of nature and meditation, others attracting those seeking, and usually finding, a Huxley-style high. If you're looking for a more active trip you'll find fishing, kayaking scuba diving, windsurfing, hiking, hang-gliding, mountain biking and riding on offer. If you have time, visit the nature reserve of San Buenaventura which comprises 100 hectares of forest abundant with birds, orchids and butterflies.
Lake Atitlán, Western Highlands
www.visitguatemala.com

Aldous Huxley (1894–1963) was born into an intellectual family of biologists and writers.

Aldous Huxley   Guatemala

It's one of the most awe-inspiring sights in the world—a huge azure lake fringed with Indian villages, mountains and pine forests, and guarded by three towering volcanoes stretching more than 3,000 metres skywards. Occupying the crater of an extinct volcano, Lake Atitlán, now 26 kilometres long and 400 metres deep, was formed around 85,000 years ago when a massive eruption cast rocks as far afield as Panama. A chug from shore to shore is one of most leisurely and spectacular boat trips you're ever likely to experience.

It was all too much for Aldous Huxley, who visited this lake in 1933 as part of a trip around Mexico, Belize and Guatemala. "Lake Como", he observed, "touches the limit of the permissibly picturesque; but Atitlán is Como with the additional embellishment of several immense volcanoes. It is really too much of a good thing". Understandably, tour operators usually prefer to misquote Huxley, claiming he called Atitlán "the most beautiful lake in the world".

Despite the aesthetic overload, Huxley's Central American jaunt proved productive, resulting in the 1934 travelogue, *Beyond the Mexique Bay*. The volume is an individualistic account of Meso-American culture, taking in everything from ancient Mayan ruins to contemporary Indian society. It's now regarded as a travel classic.

The work is just one of 47 books by Huxley, who led a famously itinerant and varied life: he lived in England, France, Italy and the US, was a fervent pacifist and humanitarian, enjoyed a spell as a Hollywood scriptwriter, and was a proponent of mysticism and experimented with hallucinogenic drugs. Many of his novels were speculative forays into utopian worlds where science and commerce sparked disturbing social consequences—remarkably apposite today.

Lake Atitlán is definitely worth a visit and is a particularly good spot to re-charge your batteries after a strenuous stint of trekking or peak-bagging. You've a choice of 13 Indian villages—each producing textiles, jewellery and baskets, and even boasting different languages—making it easy to find a quiet cabana and enjoy the lake's curious tranquillity. It's also the perfect place to reflect on Huxley's ability to meld social theory with compelling narrative, science with art, and philosophy with logic. As one of the greatest thinkers and commentators of his day, his work proves you can never really have too much of a good thing.

Italy's Como or Garda? The US's Tahoe or Siberia's Baikal? There are many contenders for the accolade of "most beautiful lake in the world". According to Aldous Huxley, this Central American marvel beggars belief.

Left: "The most remarkable thing about these Indian costumes is that they are not Indian at all, but old European. Little scraps of seventeenth and eighteenth-century Spain have been caught here and miraculously preserved, like flies in the hard amber of primitive conservatism." *Beyond the Mexique Bay*.
Following double page: Lake Atitlán is 26 km long and 400 m deep.

Arthur Conan Doyle (1859–1930). Many Sherlock Holmes stories were serialised in the UK's *The Strand* magazine. When Doyle decided to kill off his detective in 1893, twenty thousand readers cancelled their subscription.

Arthur Conan Doyle England

HOW TO GET THERE

The nearest airport is Exeter, around 25 km to the east of Dartmoor, and there are regular buses running from the city across the moor. The B3212 west from Exeter will take you close to Grimspound and other key locations. Dartmoor covers nearly 600 km² of wilderness and is home to Europe's largest collection of Stone Age sites. It also offers good hiking, fishing and horse riding and is best explored by foot, although you should make sure you are well equipped as the weather can change rapidly. Don't miss the High Moorland Visitor Centre in Princetown; formerly the Duchy Hotel, it's where Doyle starting writing *The Hound of the Baskervilles*.
Dartmoor National Park, Devon
www.sherlockholmesonline.org | www.discoverdartmoor.com

Our tale begins, as all good murder mysteries should, beside a blazing hearth. It's 1901 in Cromer, England, and the journalist Bertram Fletcher-Robinson is regaling Arthur Conan Doyle with tales from Devon, the county where he spent his youth. In the 17th century, his story went, the squire Richard Cabell brutally attacked his wife one night on Dartmoor, suspecting her of infidelity. During her death throes, her faithful dog ripped out the killer's throat before dying under his blade. From then on, the phantom hound has roamed the moor, savaging Cabell's descendents whenever they dared walk alone at night.

Doyle needed little encouragement. A few weeks later the duo were exploring Dartmoor's sweeping terrain, trekking to tors and remote prehistoric settlements on foot. They also covered miles by horse and carriage—courtesy of the Fletcher-Robinsons' driver, one Henry Baskerville. The result was perhaps the most famous Sherlock Holmes story, *The Hound of the Baskervilles*.

The gothic mystery was serialised in *The Strand* magazine in 1901–1902 to instant acclaim, boosting the publication's circulation by more than 30,000. The success was well-timed. A doctor-turned-writer, Doyle was constantly pursuing new avenues, but since 1893—when he had killed off Holmes to focus on historical novels—life had been far from easy. He ran unsuccessfully for Parliament and his wife fell terminally ill with tuberculosis. He also served a tough stint as a field doctor in the Boer War. By 1901, Doyle's finances were in a parlous state. Resurrecting Holmes presented the perfect solution. Cunningly, the writer set the story prior to the Holmes' demise at the Reichenbach Falls in *The Final Problem*.

When you visit Dartmoor, you'll find it easy to walk in Doyle's footsteps. Visit Fox Tor Mire, and you'll be standing at the book's treacherous Grimpen Mire peat bog. The Bronze Age settlement of Grimspound is the inspiration for Holmes' hide-out, while Baskerville Hall is harder to track down: Buckfastleigh's Hayford Hall and Brook Manor, and Okehampton's Lewtrenchard Manor, are all contenders.

As with all good murder mysteries, there's a final twist. Fletcher Robinson died in 1907 at just 36. The official cause of death was peritonitis, but at least five other theories have been mooted. The truth? The journalist had penned much of the narrative, the conspiracy theorists claimed, and Doyle was so keen to conceal his brazen plagiarism that he poisoned the book's real author. Preposterous though the story sounds, it's one Conan Doyle mystery that may never be solved.

On a sunny day Dartmoor is a benign landscape of granite outcrops, heather and babbling brooks. But visit this English moor on a foggy night, and you'll be in a world of craggy silhouettes and ghoulish howls: a fitting home for a spectral hound.

Left: The hound guarding the entrance to Dartmoor's
Hayford Hall, thought to have been the inspiration
for Baskerville Hall.
Above: Princetown, home to Dartmoor Prison.
Following double page: "Behind the peaceful and sunlit
countryside there rose, dark against the evening sky,
the long, gloomy curve of the moor, broken by the
jagged and sinister hills." Dr Watson's description
of Dartmoor in *The Hound of the Baskervilles*.

Christian Marclay (1955–) with his record player-cum-guitar.

HOW TO GET THERE

The nearest international airports are JFK, situated towards the east of New York in Queens, and Newark, in New Jersey, situated to the west. Both airports are connected by bus to Manhattan's Grand Central Station, Port Authority Bus Terminal, and Penn Station. The speediest way to get to the East Village is via the subway, which runs 24 hours a day: take the no. 6 (IRT Lexington Avenue) to Astor Place or the R or W (BMT lines) to 8th Street. The Stone is a not-for-profit performance space, and Marclay performs there around once a month. The artist is represented by New York's Paula Cooper Gallery. The Stone, Corner of Avenue C and Second Street, The East Village, Manhattan, New York www.thestonenyc.com | www.mcachicago.org/cm_media/run-index.htm

Christian Marclay United States

As creative breeding grounds go, New York's East Village must rank as one of the world's most fecund. Allan Ginsberg lived here—his house frequented by fellow Beat writers Jack Kerouac and William Burroughs—while bands such as the Velvet Underground, the Ramones and Blondie thrashed out their proto-punk in the district's gritty clubs. It's not surprising that this potent mix of raw music-making and the avant-garde has helped produce one of the 21st-century's leading experimental artists, Christian Marclay.

Marclay arrived in the East Village in 1977, an exchange student from an art course in Boston. He spent a year at Cooper Union— a school specialising in art, architecture and engineering—and immersed himself in the thriving scene of hip-hop, punk, performance art and sound installation.

"New York was an amazing environment", commented Marclay. "I went back to Boston and felt that I should bring back that energy that I discovered there." The sojourn inspired Marclay to organise his own festival—an experimental mélange of performance art and punk rock—and gave birth to his own famous style. Lacking musical training and an instrument, the artist adapted a record player and wore it slung guitar-style over his shoulder. He then formed a duo: guitarist Kurt Henry

provided the chords, while Marclay "scratched" out the backing rhythm on vinyl records liberated from second-hand record shops.

By 1980, Marclay was back in New York for good. Record-strewn installations, photo- and video-montage, further turntable-powered performances, four-metre-high drum kits, and silicone-rubber bass guitars followed, the relationship between sound and visuals being the ever-present stimulus for Marclay's output.

To see Marclay's mix-and-match aesthetic taken to almost maniacal extremes, check out his 2002 piece *Video Quartet*. The work comprises a fast-moving stream-of-consciousness montage of classic Hollywood film clips, set to a spliced soundtrack. It's a sublime piece of work, a visual and aural assault that evokes memories, in-jokes and cultural references at a breakneck pace, both bewildering and entrancing the viewer.

While gentrification may have rubbed smooth some of the East Village's grungy edges, the melting pot that inspired Marclay can still be found. When you visit don't miss Alphabet City towards the east of the district, still home to the kind of record stores that provided Marclay with his raw materials. If you're lucky, you can catch the man performing at The Stone—a venue that's keeping the East Village avant-garde scene very much alive.

How did a sculpture student become one of the world's most famous experimental artists? Visit the boho district of Manhattan's East Village to find out.

Below: Christian Marclay, *Sound Sheet*, 1991.
Right: Christian Marclay, *Video Quartet*, 2002.

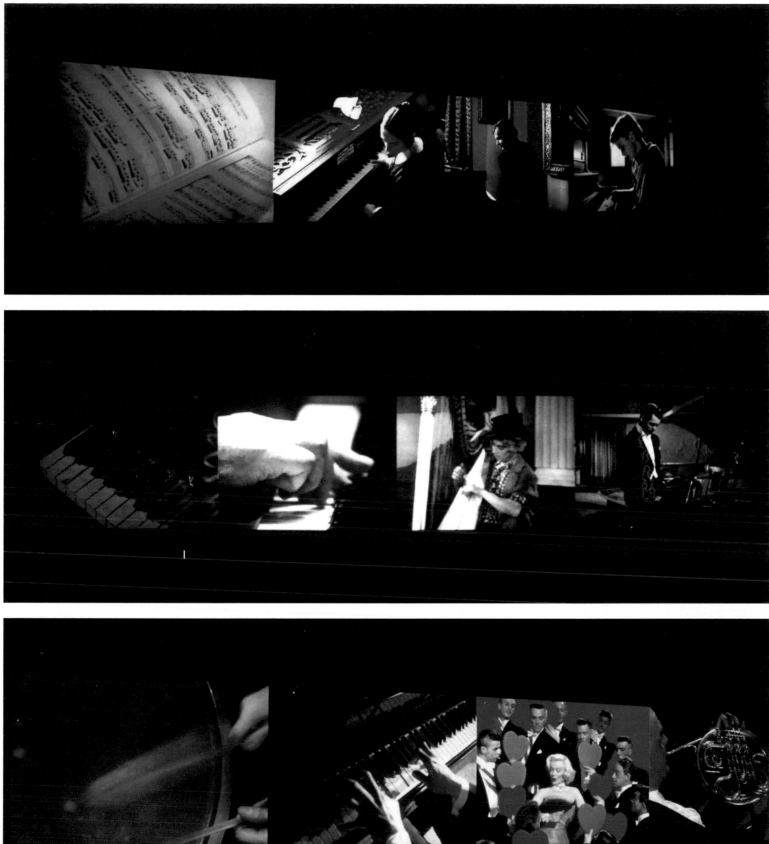

Julio Osorio (1971–).

Julio Osorio Latin America

HOW TO GET THERE

Following in Julio Osorio's footsteps is easy to organise. Much of Central and South America is well served by flights and long distances buses. If you want a helping hand with your trip, Journey Latin America (www.journeylatinamerica. co.uk) should be able to put together a good itinerary. Colombia is one of the most beautiful countries in South America, a land of stunning Caribbean beaches, jungles, mountains and lowland plains plus some of the best coffee in the world. Sadly, its reputation for cocaine trafficking, warring guerrillas and paramilitary groups, organised crime and kidnapping makes it less attractive to tourists. However, security has been stepped up in recent years and some areas have been deemed lower risk destinations. Children of the Andes helps youngsters affected by violence and poverty through education, health, protection and peace-building initiatives. Osorio's photographs are available in his book *Work, Play and No Rest*.

Central and South America

www.workplayandnorest.com | www.childrenoftheandes.org
www.savethechildren.org/countries/latin_america_caribbean/index.asp
www.comminit.com/papers/p_0011.html

Machu Picchu, Iguaçu Falls, the Perito Moreno glacier, Rio de Janeiro: the list of must-see destinations in Latin America is recited like a mantra in backpacking circles. But for Julio Osorio, such attractions held little allure; instead he plotted a route via some of Central and South America's most poverty-stricken towns and cities. The result is a moving collection of photographs, depicting everyday life for some of the most deprived children on the continent.

Osorio left Colombia at 13, moving to England to eventually become an established photographer. At 29, he decided to re-visit his home country in an attempt to capture scenes redolent of his childhood. Over five years, Osorio backpacked through Colombia, Mexico and Venezuela, and even made a detour to the shanty towns of South Africa, taking candid photographs of children throughout his journey. Unusually, he chose not to focus on child sweatshops or starving toddlers, but uplifting scenes of laughter and levity.

"The standard coverage of these issues is about poverty, misery, anguish and sadness", commented Osorio, who completed his trip in 2004. "I wanted to capture the beauty of childhood with the poverty around." The photographs chronicle all aspects of life for youngsters in Latin America, from five-year-olds begging on the streets to teenagers playing in the surf, working in markets, or selling goods on tourist buses. Osorio eschewed posed compositions and honed a reportage style for the project.

"When I went home I realised how much I missed the place", said the photographer. "It was a familiar sight, seeing kids working but still smiling and playing. I wanted to show people that you don't necessarily need money to be a happy person, and that happiness comes from little things rather than having a Game Boy."

Of all the places visited by Osorio in Colombia, the Caribbean port of Cartagena is a good place to join his trail. Regarded as one of the most tourist-friendly areas in the country, it boasts a stunning walled city, colonial architecture, and a good collection of art galleries and museums. Nearby is Parque Tayrona, a national park once inhabited by Tayrona Indians. Inevitably, you don't have to travel far to find the less well-off: half of Cartagena's population lives below the poverty line, many having been displaced from their coffee plantations by guerrillas. To avoid becoming a "poverty tourist", you could support one of the charities for children, such as the Bogotá-based Children of the Andes or the Cartagena-based El Colegio del Cuerpo.

Tours around shanty towns and former warn-torn enclaves are booming. But are such trips anything more than voyeuristic "poverty tourism"? This Colombian photographer tackled the moral conundrum with his lens.

Right and following double page: Julio attempted to capture all aspects of the lives of South America children. According to the children's aid agency UNICEF, sixty per cent of Latin America's children are living in poverty.

Georg Guðni (1961–) has exhibited and sold his works worldwide.

HOW TO GET THERE

Iceland's main airport is Keflavik International, a 45-minute drive from the capital Reykjavik. In summer you can also reach the country by ferry from Norway, Denmark, the Shetland Islands and the Faroe Islands. There is no railway but the bus services are good in the summer. The Snæfellsjökull National Park is situated around 120 km north of the capital, and is accessed via National Road 574, known as Útnesvegur. The Central Highlands are best explored by guided tour in a four-wheel drive. Iceland offers a broad variety of activities including trekking, bathing in hot springs, midnight golf, bird-watching and whale-spotting, while the capital offers a thriving arts scene and nightlife. Gudni exhibits at several Reykjavik galleries including Galleri Lars Bohman (www.gallerilarsbohman.com). *Strange Familiar—The Work of Georg Guðni* (Perceval Press) is a compilation of the artist's work.
www.georggudni.com | www.icetourist.is

Georg Gudni Iceland

Most visitors to Iceland are attracted by its stunning terrain: beyond verdant valleys and woodlands lie frozen landscapes of fjords and rough lava fields, hot springs and the largest glaciers in Europe. But for Georg Guðni, "everyday" scenes of fog-bound valleys, rocks and endless horizons made far more enticing subjects.

Born in Reykjavik, Guðni spent much of his childhood exploring Iceland's vast interior, accompanying his geologist father on surveying expeditions. At the end of his fine-art studies in Holland he eschewed the conceptual and "new expressionism" paths of his peers, and took up landscape painting using traditional oils. "Everybody was chasing the new thing", commented Guðni, "but I didn't want to be always running after the crowds. I started to look around me and what moved me strongly was the landscapes".

The decision proved controversial: many critics, and even Guðni himself regarded landscape painting, with its heyday in the 19th-century, as *passé*. "It was almost like a forbidden path", continued Guðni. "I was going backwards in time, into calmness, doing things carefully and with attention to detail." The artist's work lay hidden for nine months before he dared show it. "The reaction was mixed. Some thought I was nuts."

In contrast to traditional landscape artists, Guðni chose not to accurately portray his environment, but tried to "capture the invisible"—the rain, fog and the layered history of the terrain—through painstakingly applied accretions of oils. He travelled throughout Iceland for inspiration, but visited places far from the tourist trail such as Gullfoss and Geysir, found some 100 kilometres east of Reykjavik. The resulting brooding skies and ethereal horizons convey a sense of timelessness, evoking the spirit of Iceland far better than any figurative study.

When planning your trip, you'll find the Snæfellsjökull National Park, situated in the far west, is a good place to start. Its landscape is hugely varied, running from the towering Snæfellsjökull glacier, volcanoes and steep mountains to the coastal plains of the seashore, teeming with wildlife. Or if it's true isolation you're after, head for the Central Highlands—a region that has never been inhabited by humans and where you can spend days without seeing a soul. It's awe-inspiring territory featuring glacial rivers, lively geothermal fields and the Víti (Hell) lake. While travelling, you might want to bear Guðni's approach in mind. "Don't go from A to B", advised the artist. "The travel itself should be a part of it: every moment of every day."

Much modern-day travel focuses on the destination rather than the journey. For this Icelandic artist, the beauty lies in "the ordinary places in between".

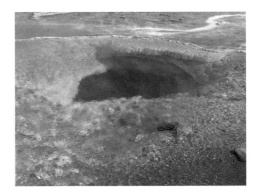

Above: The landscape of Iceland has inspired other artists: the Snaefellsjökull glacier is mentioned in Jules Verne's book, *Journey to the Centre of the Earth* and Tolkien drew on the myths of Iceland to create Middle-earth.
Right: Guðni's paintings are the very antithesis of tourist-friendly works, depicting inclement weather and landscapes traditionally overlooked by visitors. "People are always going to a certain place, but 99 per cent of nature is between these places: people are not interested in them."

John Ronald Reuel Tolkien (1892–1973). Both Tolkien and Lewis are buried in Oxford: Lewis at Holy Trinity Church, Headington; and Tolkein at Wolvercote Cemetery.

HOW TO GET THERE

The nearest airports are Birmingham International, Heathrow, Gatwick and Luton. Try to land at Heathrow, which offers the quickest coach connections to the city (around 1 hr 20 mins). The city is also connected to London by the M40 motorway (exit at junctions 8 or 9), and there are frequent trains and coaches taking around an hour from central London. You'll find the Eagle and Child on St Giles', a wide road leading north from the centre of the city, around ten minutes' walk from the train and bus stations. Oxford is home to one of the world's oldest and most prestigious universities and offers a wealth of architectural and cultural riches. While you're there do visit the often overlooked Pitt Rivers Museum, a bizarre collection of ethnographic finds from shrunken heads to Inuit fur parkas, and home to the stuffed dodo that inspired Lewis Carroll to feature the creature in *Alice in Wonderland*. And if the sun is shining try your hand at punting on the Isis or Cherwell rivers.
Eagle and Child, 49 St Giles', Oxford
www.oxfordcity.co.uk | www.mythsoc.org/inklings.html

J. R. R. Tolkien, C. S. Lewis England

The Eagle and Child pub is situated on Oxford's sweeping St Giles' boulevard. Just seconds away lie the city's hallowed university colleges—centres of academic debate and rigorous analysis. But within this pub's oak-panelled walls, the mythical and mystical often took precedence: the establishment was the favourite haunt of John Ronald Reuel Tolkien and Clive Staples Lewis, authors of *The Lord of the Rings* and *The Chronicles of Narnia* respectively.

It started with the Inklings—a group of Oxford academics and writers who met to discuss works-in-progress from the 1930s to the 1960s. Members used to meet on Thursdays in C. S. Lewis' rooms at Magdalen College, while an extended group frequented this pub's "Rabbit Room" for ale-assisted sessions on Tuesdays from the early 1940s. J. R. R. Tolkien and C. S. Lewis regularly held readings within college walls, while the pub was reserved for lighter discussion and imbibing of local ales in a fug of cigarette- and pipe-smoke.

Both Oxford dons, Tolkien and Lewis met in 1926 and soon found a kinship in an ambition to break beyond scholarly works into fiction. Their pact to embark on projects exploring space and time travel resulted in Lewis' *Space Trilogy* (1935–45) and Tolkien's unfinished novel, *The Lost Road*, published

posthumously in 1987. It also gave Tolkien the impetus to complete *The Hobbit*—penned after he doodled the now-famous opening line, "in a hole in the ground there lived a hobbit", during a bored moment while marking an exam paper in 1931.

Thanks to the Inklings' critiques and encouragement, we now have the fantasy worlds of Middle-earth and Narnia, the journeys of Frodo Baggins, and the exploits of four young siblings holidaying in a country house during World War II. The resulting novels became best-sellers.

Tolkien and Lewis, alongside fellow Inklings, have since been labelled Romantic Christians, writing works that attempt to convey fundamental truths through fantasy rather than reason. The strong religious allegorical content of their novels is no coincidence: Tolkien was a Catholic, and helped convert Lewis to Christianity in 1931.

Visit the Eagle and Child today and you'll find most of its olde-worlde charm intact. An alehouse since 1650, open fires and snugs provide a good refuge for a winter pint. Sample a few pints of the locally brewed Hook Norton cask ale and it's pretty easy to conjure up those fireside sessions. And if you really want to impress locals, refer to the pub by the Inklings' preferred moniker—the Bird and Baby.

This pub in the heart of the historic city of Oxford is perennially packed, but there's always room at the bar for elves, hobbits, orcs, giants and the odd white witch.

Above and right: Outside and inside the Eagle and Child pub on Oxford's St Giles'.

Below: All Souls and Jesus College roofscape.
Below right: The Radcliffe camera.

Jorge Luis Borges (1899–1986) (centre). Alongside Gabriel García Márquez, Borges is most famous for his works of "magical realism"—narratives that combine reality with elements of surrealism and fantasy. Although the city isn't named, Borges' short story *Death and the Compass* is said to be the writer's most faithful evocation of the spirit of Buenos Aires.

HOW TO GET THERE

The nearest international airport is Ministro Pistarini (known as Ezeiza), situated 35 km south-west of the city. Café Tortoni is situated on Avenida de Mayo, in the very centre of Buenos Aires. The nearest underground (subte) train stations are Piedras on line A and Av. De Mayo on line C. Be aware that Buenos Aires is a very diffuse city and its roads are extremely long—take a bus, tube or a taxi, rather than be tempted to walk if you are travelling more than a few blocks. Café Tortoni also hosts tango and jazz shows downstairs. While you're there be sure to visit the Palermo barrio on the north-east side of Buenos Aires, home to some of the best bars, museums and parks in the city.

Café Tortoni, Avenida de Mayo 825, Centro, Buenos Aires
www.cafetortoni.com.ar
www.themodernword.com/borges/borges_news

Jorge Luis Borges   Argentina

Bristling with neoclassical facades and laced with wide, leafy boulevards, Buenos Aires owes much more to the architects and ideas of Europe than of South America. Café Tortoni, a belle-époque *confitería* that wouldn't look out of place on Paris' Rive Gauche, proves just how deep this influence runs. The establishment has hosted a million feisty intellectual debates, acting as a hub for the city's artists, politicians, writers, musicians and academics during the city's cultural boom of the early 20th century.

Founded in 1858, Tortoni is the city's oldest café and has kept the passage of time at bay remarkably successfully. Visit today and an impeccably dressed waiter will seat you at a marble-topped table. The wooden-panelled walls are adorned with gilt mirrors and monochrome portraits of the country's greatest sons and daughters, while the bar is a buttress of deep mahogany, sporting coffee machines buffed to chrome perfection by attentive baristas. Sipping your *cortado* you'll almost certainly feel compelled to puff on a Gauloise and engage a brace of strangers in an impenetrable existential debate.

The basement was the epicentre of the city's artistic revolution—the refuge where Jorge Luis Borges and assorted intellectuals met during the 1920s and 1930s to debate literature and politics. Such café sessions were critical for Borges. Although born in Buenos Aires, he spent seven years in Europe during his teens and early twenties, and returned to find a group of similarly well-travelled aesthetes, fired up by the radical ideas of Europe. Conversations ranged from the philosophy of Schopenhauer and Berkeley, to anarchism, symbolism and ultraism—a literary movement espousing radical forms which Borges had imported from Spain.

It was the perfect place for Borges to explore his favourite themes of fantasy, theology, philosophy and mythology, and absorb local and international culture. The resulting output was broad, ranging from explorations of time and identity to faithful depictions of South American life. By the 1960s Borges had established himself as one of Argentina's most celebrated writers producing poetry, screenplays and literary criticism.

While you're racking your brains for your own great work, you might note that Borges was a master of the literary forgery: the act of penning reviews of works that didn't exist. In his view, this was a far better way of expressing ideas than going to the trouble of writing an "original". In a city where convivial conversation in an elegant café surely ranks above hard work, one finds it hard to disagree.

Jorge Luis Borges is Argentina's greatest writer. Where better than to ponder his legacy than at this favourite cafe, in the heart of Buenos Aires?

Right and following double page: Bueos Aires' Café Tortoni, founded in 1858.

Joseph Conrad (1857–1924).

HOW TO GET THERE

The Democratic Republic of Congo boasts the second-largest river in the world, a stunning landscape of thick rainforest and is home to bonobos—the species of great ape that is the closest relative to humans, sharing more than 98 per cent of our DNA. But those seeking to follow Conrad's Congo trail are advised to wait. Sadly, most of the country cannot be visited due to its volatile political climate, a collapsed economy, and high levels of crime. Eastern and north-eastern parts of the country should particularly be avoided. Until this situation abates, you can always throw your energies into one of the charities that are trying to aid those affected by the conflict, such as SOS Children's Charity and the World Wildlife Fund.
www.soschildrensvillages.org.uk/children-charity.htm
www.worldwildlife.org | www.josephconrad.org

Joseph Conrad Africa

Little could prepare Joseph Conrad for the harrowing scenes of the Congo in 1890. The 32-year-old was captaining a steamer, shuttling goods along the River Congo's upper reaches for a Belgian company. As he wended through the dense equatorial rainforest, he discovered the area's natural resources of ivory and rubber were being ruthlessly plundered—largely for Belgian ruler Leopold II's personal gain—while its inhabitants were being enslaved, raped, mutilated and massacred.

The trip left Conrad mentally disturbed and physically debilitated with malaria. It also provided him with the raw materials to write one of the 20th century's most celebrated modern novellas, *Heart of Darkness*. Published in 1902, this taut psychological narrative essays the perils of colonialism, the superficiality of civilization and the corruptibility of man. Thankfully, the volume helped raise public awareness of the atrocities—little known around the world— and control was eventually wrested from King Leopold II in 1908. But by then, millions of Congolese had been butchered and the area had been bled of much of its wealth.

Conrad's river adventure was entirely in keeping with a life of high drama. Born Józef Teodor Konrad Korzeniowski to an aristocratic family in Russian Poland, he was orphaned at

eleven, joined the French merchant navy at 16, and speedily became embroiled in two murky plots: gun-running in Marseille and a bid to put the Duke of Madrid on the Spanish throne. By 21, he had taught himself English and joined the British merchant navy, going on to spend 16 years sailing to India, Singapore, Australia, Borneo, Sumatra and, of course, the Congo.

Sadly, a century on, the lot of the Congolese remains tragic. Now known as the Democratic Republic of Congo, the area gained its independence from Belgium in 1960 but at the time of writing, was still rife with bloodshed, famine and corruption. A five-year civil war broke out in 1998, killing an estimated four million people, and the ensuing fragile peace has been broken by bouts of military action and civil unrest. Just as in Conrad's day, the conflict is largely over control of the country's vast natural resources, particularly its wealth of diamonds, gold, cobalt and copper.

Conrad's own life had a happier ending. A naturalised British citizen, Conrad gave up the sea in 1894, aged 37, to take up writing full-time, married and settled in the UK. His exploits fuelled more than thirty books, novels and numerous short stories.

The place: the River Congo, in deepest Africa. The scene: Joseph Conrad is at the helm of the Roi des Belges, chugging into the heart of King Leopold II's brutal regime.

Right: A 1911 postcard showing ivory trading in the Congo.

Following double page: Modern-day views of the River Congo.

Photographie R. Visser, Déposé.

Congo.
No. 28.   L'achat d'Jvoire.

Gordon Jackson in Alexander Mackendrick's *Whisky Galore!*, 1949.

HOW TO GET THERE

The nearest major airport is Glasgow, which runs connecting flights to Barra, situated 8 km south of Eriskay, and Benbecula, 53 km to the north. Eriskay is connected to Barra by boat (50 mins) and to Benbecula by bus (90 mins). If you want to avoid plane travel, take a boat from Oban on Scotland's west coast. You've a choice of two routes from here: a ferry to Lochboisdale on South Uist followed by a drive to Eriskay (20 mins) or a ferry to Barra and then a connecting boat. Eriskay is part of a chain of islands known as The Uists. The island is just 2.4 km by 4 km and offers some accommodation, a shop and a post office, and of course a pub. The Outer Hebrides is a 210-km-long archipelago, regarded as some of the most unspoilt islands in the world. Activities include sailing, walking, bird- and wildlife-watching—and escaping the rat race. Those keen to separate fact from fiction should read Roger Hutchinson's book, *Polly: The True Story Behind "Whisky Galore"*.

Eriskay, Outer Hebrides
www.undiscoveredscotland.co.uk/eriskay/eriskay
www.guidetotheuists.co.uk/getting_there.htm
www.isle-of-eriskay.com

Alexander Mackendrick   Scotland

Visit the tiny island of Eriskay off the west coast of Scotland, and take a stroll along its northern shores. If you're extremely lucky, you might find a rare piece of history buried in its white sands: a bottle of whisky spilled from the SS Politician, a cargo ship wrecked during a fierce storm in 1941.

The freighter was carrying some 264,000 bottles of quality Scotch from Liverpool to Jamaica when it smashed against the rocks of the Sound of Eriskay. The islanders needed little encouragement: driven to despair by a war-induced whisky drought, they took to their boats and liberated an estimated 24,000 bottles before Customs and Excise officers halted the free-for-all. The extraordinary episode inspired Compton Mackenzie's novel *Whisky Galore!*, subsequently made into a film by the UK's Ealing Studios in 1949.

The movie is a masterpiece of melodramatic comedy replete with thick Scottish brogue, crofters' cottages lit by flickering candlelight, crashing North Atlantic breakers, and a community half-crazed by the scarcity of its favourite tipple. The Hebrideans' hammed-up stoicism is hugely entertaining, while the authorities are depicted with a Keystone Cops-style irreverence.

As for the film's setting, we have Alexander Mackendrick to thank for its verisimilitude.

The director and co-writer insisted on shooting the entire film in the Outer Hebrides, choosing Barra, Eriskay's larger neighbour, as the location. Craigstone village hall became the impromptu studio, and many of the island's inhabitants made willing extras. Co-writer Compton Mackenzie, a former Barra resident, even managed to secure a cameo appearance.

Visit Eriskay today, and you'll find it has retained much of the raw isolation of those war years. Although linked by a causeway to the neighbouring island of South Uist in 2000, it remains famous for its unspoilt beaches, rugged landscape, bracing walks and abundant wildlife including herons, golden eagles, sea otters, dolphins and whales. The resident population stands at less than 130.

When you visit, make sure you call in at the Am Politician, Eriskay's only pub. There'll you'll find a bottle of the famous contraband—sadly not for sale—plus newspaper cuttings and photographs proving that real-life events were not quite as light-hearted as the film suggests. In reality, the custom officers' search revealed several stashes of the liquid haul, there were clashes and several islanders were incarcerated for theft. Such unsettling detail surely calls for a steadying dram or two.

A real life shipwreck inspired this classic Ealing comedy. Head for Scotland's Outer Hebrides for a real taste of Scotch on the rocks.

Above: Maurice Watson, then a 17-year-old deck cadet on the SS Politician when it hit rocks in 1941, returned to the island in 2006: "It was filthy weather: blowing a gale, a big sea, the lot. We took evasive action but the stern was caught on a rock and the bow in sand. We knew from the time the ship struck that it was going to be lost." Right and following double page: Eriskay is famous for being the first piece of Scottish soil visited by Bonnie Prince Charlie, who landed here in 1745 and went on to raise his Jacobite army in the islands and Highlands of Scotland.

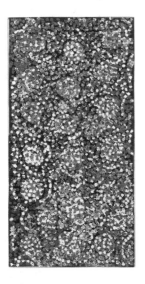

Papunya Tula Australia

HOW TO GET THERE

The nearest airport is situated 14 km south of Alice Springs. You can hire a four-wheel drive, but a good way to explore the outback is with a guided tour; you'll find a plethora of options—including ballooning, camel rides, horse treks and camping trips—run from Alice Springs. For good Aboriginal art, visit Papunya Tula Artists on Todd St in Alice Springs or two good community arts centres: Ikuntji Art Centre at Haasts Bluff (permit required), situated 230 km west of the city, and Warlukurlangu Artists at Yuendumu, found 270 north-west. Wayward Bus (www.waywardbus.com.au) also runs art trips to remote communities. And if you're keen on acquiring a work of art but don't fancy the trek, visit Aboriginal Art Online (www.aboriginalartonline.com), which works with community arts centres.

The Red Centre, Northern Territory, Central Australia
www.papunyatula.com.au | www.atn.com.au/nt/south/parks-e.htm
www.aboriginal-art.de/art_deu/kunst.htm

This is a story of cruel cultural meddling and life-affirming art. In 1960, Robert Menzies' government established the settlement of Papunya in Australia's Northern Territory. It soon became home to hundreds of Aboriginal people, forcibly moved from their tribal lands across the outback because the government wanted to "westernise" nomadic people in state-controlled communities.

The project was a disaster. Housing was overcrowded and conditions were poor. Disease was rife and Aboriginal culture suppressed. Most disturbing of all, children of mixed parentage were taken from their families and placed into foster care or government institutions—a practice that dated from the earliest days of colonisation and continued until the mid-1960s. But 1971 marked a turning point. Art teacher Geoff Bardon was posted to Papunya and noticed that children were still drawing traditional designs in the sand. Rustling up school art supplies, he encouraged the youngsters to reproduce the designs of their forbears. The elders followed suit, going on to acquire canvases, and the Western Desert art movement was born, with Papunya Tula established as an artist-owned cooperative.

Papunya Tula boasted some thirty founding members, with Turkey Tolson Tjupurrula, Johnny Warangkula Tjupurrula and Clifford Possum Tjapaltjarri among the group's most famous pioneers. Their work was based on Aboriginal "dreamings"—stories passed from generation to generation to illuminate the inextricable relationship between people and their land, the elements, animals and plant life. The paintings are often interpreted as aerial landscapes: multi-coloured swirls and patchworks evoking desert hills, sacred trails and fertile plains, but in reality they contain layers of complex symbolic meaning. Dots are often a feature: now considered emblematic of Aboriginal art, some historians believe they were first used to obscure sacred symbols. Papunya Tula work is now exhibited throughout the world, with paintings selling for up to several hundred thousand dollars.

Although many remote Aboriginal communities still suffer from high unemployment, poor housing and ill-health, misguided cultural assimilation programmes are thankfully a thing of the past. The land rights movement of the early 1970s put large tracts back under Aboriginal control, and many Aboriginal people have now moved back to their homelands. Many areas are therefore out of bounds for travellers without an official permit, but you can visit its national parks—which are vast enough to tire even the most energetic.

Aboriginal art stretches back 30,000 years, but recent western interest has created a booming market worth millions of dollars. Disturbing events in Australia's outback provided the catalyst for change.

Left: Johnny Warangkula Tjupurrula, *Water-Tjukurrpa*, 1998. Acrylic on canvas, 182.5 x 91 cm.
Right, above: Mick Namarari Tjapaltjarri, *No Title*, 1996. Acrylic on canvas, 59.5 x 89.5 cm.
Right, below: Nyurapayia Nampitjinpa, *No Title*, 1999. Acrylic on canvas, 91 x 136 cm.

Following double page: The spectacular deserts of the Red Centre are home to eroded mountain ranges, ochre pits and gorges, and the Tnorula creater—formed when a comet crashed to Earth 140 million years ago. One of the biggest draws is Australia's greatest natural attraction, Ayers Rock, also known by its Aboriginal name, Uluru.

"What's amazing about climate change is that it's partly a cultural phenomenon", commented David Buckland, director of Cape Farewell. "It happens at the rate it does because of the cars we drive and the fossil fuels we burn. The science we can't change, but the culture we can."

Cape Farewell High Arctic

HOW TO GET THERE

Flying to the High Artic, or indeed anywhere, will only hasten the demise of this destination, and there have been many critics of tourism in the area. That said, there are a number of eco-conscious cruise operators, and the summer season from June to September offers the broadest selection of routes. Discover the World runs cruises in the Arctic using relatively small ships (carrying a maximum of one hundred people) and also employs local guides. In summer you can also reach the archipelago by boat from Tromsø in northern Norway (two to three days). Trips attract wildlife watchers and photographers, plus those seeking a glimpse of pristine ice floes and the Northern Lights. Alternatively, for a cleaner conscience and a healthier bank balance, try to track down David Hinton's film Art from the Arctic, a record of all three voyages, or visit the touring exhibition of the work, The Ship: The Art of Climate Change. Spitsbergen Archipelago, Svalbard, High Arctic www.capefarewell.com | www.discover-arctic.co.uk

They endured temperatures of minus 22°F, sea sickness and encounters with many a peckish polar bear. They met the frozen landscape with indignation, incredulity, resignation and plain white fear. And some 2,500 nautical miles and three expeditions later, they delivered a host of extraordinary works including a projection of the death of an iceberg, a sonic work of creaking and melting ice, startling phrases projected onto floes, and the naming of a newly discovered island.

The project was Cape Farewell, an ambitious programme designed to communicate the issues of climate change through art, science and education. The first voyage set sail in 2003: a crew of artists, journalists, film-makers, scientists and educationalists boarded the Noorderlicht, a century-old Dutch schooner, and weaved through the towering icebergs of the Svalbard Archipelago in the High Arctic. That first voyage from Tromsø to Spitsbergen was followed by two further expeditions around Spitsbergen in 2004 and 2005. The crew numbered writers Ian McEwan and Gretel Ehrlich, while the artists included Antony Gormley, Gary Hume, Rachel Whiteread, Alex Hartley, Gautier Deblonde and David Buckland.

To throw the issue of climate change into sharp relief, the boat navigated routes that had

previously been inaccessible, but were now open due to melting ice. While the artists were busy creating works using photography, video, prose, sculpture and sound, the scientists analysed water, studying temperatures, plankton life and levels of salinity.

"To some people climate change is on such a monumental scale they think, well, if the ice is melting in Greenland, so what?" commented David Buckland, artist and director of Cape Farewell. "We intended to use artworks to communicate our understanding of climate change on a human scale."

Spitsbergen is regarded as one of the world's last remaining true wildernesses: a land of huge glaciers and towering fjords inhabited by reindeer, arctic foxes, walruses, whales, seals and polar bears. To preserve this awe-inspiring environment, scientists estimate that we need to reduce carbon- dioxide emissions by some sixty per cent globally within the next twenty years in order to prevent temperatures, and water levels, rising further.

Although faced with hard evidence of global warming—and the possibility of no summer ice at the North Pole by the mid-21st century—most artists remained positive. "Most were hopeful we can achieve cultural change", added Buckland. "I can't wait to get back. It's like nothing else up there."

Facts and figures are a critical part of the climate-change debate, but they often fail to communicate the stark truths of global warming. So what happens if you sail a group of artists into the thick of melting ice floes?

Right, top left: David Buckland, Ice Texts, 2004–5.
Right, top right: David Buckland, The Pregnant Messenger, 2005.
Right, bottom: Cape Farewell artists included (front row) Max Eastley, Nick Edwards, Antony Gormley, Siobhan Davies, Gautier Deblonde, Tom Wakeford, Dan Harvey; (back row) Charlie Kronick, Alex Hartley, Peter Clegg, Rachel Whiteread, David Buckland, Heather Ackroyd, Ian McEwan.
Following double page:
Left: Heather Ackroyd and Dan Harvey, Ice Lens, 2005.
Right: A view across the Svalbaard Archipelago in the High Arctic.

The Monte Baldo hotel sits on the edge of Italy's spectacular Lake Garda (far left). Cradle Mountain Huts runs "minimum impact" walking tours through Tasmania (left and right).

LAIDBACK LEISURE
Ireland
Tour the quiet lanes and valleys of Ireland in a one-horse-power caravan. Mayo Horsedrawn Caravans sleep four, and little equestrian experience is required. Don't forget to pack a musical instrument—you can take part in jamming sessions in pubs en route. From €650/$770 per week.
www.horsedrawn.mayonet.com

Italy
Monte Baldo is an old-style, chic hotel found on the west shore of Lake Garda, Italy's purest lake. Campari and soda on the terrace, swimming, tennis and boat trips across the water guarantee *la dolce vita*. From €62/$79 per night.
www.hotelmontebaldo.it

Canada
This oceanfront resort is a good base for whale-watching, star gazing, deep-sea fishing and beachcombing. Long Beach Lodge Resort provides a choice of lodge rooms and rainforest cottages, and more adventurous types can hike, surf and scuba dive. From €108/$129 per night.
www.longbeachlodgeresort.com

China
Looking for a place with a sea view? These tree houses are perched in tamarind trees on the island of Hainan in the South China Sea. An unspoilt beach and a 2,000-hectare Buddhist park are but a stone's throw away. Temples and silence abounds. From €23/$27 per night.
www.treehousesofhawaii.com/nanshan.html

Argentina
Saddle up or just kick back at this family-run *estancia*, set among 1,200 hectares of open valley and woodlands in Argentina's Central Sierras. La Constancia is a good base for trekking and horse riding, or just indulging in the country's legendary steak and red wine. From €82/$100 per night.
www.laconstancia.net

India
Ayurvedic massage and strong coffee may not sound the ideal combination, but this Kerala homestay pulls its off. The Tranquil retreat is tucked away on a vanilla bean plantation in the middle of a rainforest, and comprises just eight rooms and a luxury treehouse. From €130/$158 per night.
www.tranquilresort.com

ACTION & ADVENTURE
Canary Islands
This remote volcanic island offers great hiking through unspoilt valleys and forests, plus a sprinkling of isolated beaches. Hotel Ibo Alfaro, a small converted country house, is a good base in the island's verdant north. From €70/$83 per night.
www.lascasascanarias.com

Tasmania
Escape the trappings of civilisation by exploring the mountains, lakes, rainforests and beaches of the Tasmanian wilderness. These eco-friendly, "minimum impact" guided walks include hut and lodge accommodation, hot showers and food. From €1085/$1291 per trek.
www.cradlehuts.com.au

Australia
The Bungle Bungle Range boasts extraordinary striped beehive-shaped domes—shaped by 20 million years' worth of erosion—plus Aboriginal art and more than 130 bird species. Hikers, photographers and wilderness fans can camp at Walardi or Kurrajong. From €7/$9 per night.
www.calm.wa.gov.au
www.kimberleywilderness.com.au

Belize
Tropical rainforests, Caribbean coral reefs, Mayan ruins and the world's only jaguar sanctuary are within half an hour of this eco-lodge, which comprises thatched cabanas right on the beach. Part of Jaguar Reef Lodge's profits go to local conservation and wildlife protection groups too. From €105/$125 per night.
www.jaguarreef.com

Kenya
Spend your days on the trail of elephants, lions, leopards and cheetahs, and repair to a luxury cottage with stunning views of Mount Kenya. Borana Ranch also runs forestry, health and education projects benefitting the local community. From €409/$495 per night.
www.borana.co.ke

Norway
These self-guided "inn-to-inn" Nordic treks take you through Captain Scott's old training ground. You'll wend through Ice-Age highlands, forests, mountains, lakes and the world's longest fjord. Bed-and-breakfast accommodation, evening meals, bus and train transfers and detailed maps are included. From €1,086/$1,297 for an 8-day trek.
www.sherpa-walking-holidays.co.uk/tours/inntoinn/jnorc.asp

Thailand

Thought Thailand was all backpackers and non-stop beach parties? Tell Tale Travel offers tailor-made itineraries, taking you off the beaten track and into the homes and culture of the locals. Trek the jungles, visit hill tribes, scrub an elephant or mix with the movers and shakers in Bangkok. Good family adventures on offer too.
From €576/$700 per week.
www.telltaletravel.co.uk

Jordan

Follow in the hoofsteps of Lawrence of Arabia on a 2-week horse trek with Unicorn Trails. You'll ride 330 km from the dunes of the central eastern Jordanian desert to the canyons of Wadi Rum. Camps are set up on en route, while the trip also includes a visit to Petra, and snorkeling and swimming in the Red and Dead Seas.
From €2,736/$3,321 for 15 days.
www.unicorntrails.com

Argentina

This hillside lodge is on the doorstep of the Parque Nacional Perito Moreno, home to one of the world's few remaining advancing glaciers. America del Sur is run by an energetic bunch, happy to book excursions, transport, and accommodation for your next leg. En suite bathrooms and under-floor heating too.
From €5/$6.5 per night.
www.americahostel.com.ar

The Azores

This is as close to swashbuckling on the high seas as you can get. Tall Ship Adventures runs trips around the unspoilt North Atlantic archipelago of the Azores on a 60-metre square-rigged brig. You'll be part of the crew but no sailing experience is required. Jaunts around the UK, the Caribbean and the Italian Riviera are also offered.
From €656/$834 for seven nights.
www.tallships.org

METROLANDS
Poland

Rivalling Prague and Vienna in architectural gems, Kraków offers cellar bars, medieval squares and scores of galleries and museums. The old town's Pollera Hotel is a good starting point for exploring this European accession country.
From €80/$95 per night.
www.pollera.com.pl

United States

San Francisco's Red Victorian B&B, situated in Haight Ashbury, keeps the Summer of Love alive with a warm welcome from Sami Sunchild, a peace café and a green policy on everything from buying local produce to recycling.
From €60/$72 per night.
www.redvic.com

Estonia

Tallinn is one of Europe's most intriguing capitals, bearing the legacy of occupation by Danes, Swedes, Poles, Lithuanians, Russians and Germans. The Olevi Residents hotel puts you at the heart of this buzzy coastal world-heritage city.
From €70/$83 per night.
www.olevi.ee

Nepal

The capital city of Kathmandu is a bustling hub of temples, pagodas, blind alleys and bazaars sitting beneath the Himalayas. The smart Hotel Vajra, surrounded by trees and gardens, provides respite from the urban frenzy. Look out for the ceiling frescos and a rooftop garden, and bag a room in the farmhouse if you can.
From €12/$14 per night.
www.hotelvajra.com

Antony Gormley (1950–). Gormley's most famous work is the *Angel of the North*—a 20-metre-high figure with a 54-metre wingspan erected in Gateshead in northern England.

HOW TO GET THERE

The nearest international airport is Perth, where you can pick up connecting flights to Kalgoorlie. For a better view of Western Australia, take the Prospector train, which will take you the 600 km east from Perth in six hours. From Kalgoorlie, take a bus the remaining 132 km north-west to Menzies (1.5 hours). Lake Ballard is around 55 km north of Menzies—which you'll cover by hire car or on an organised trip.

Inside Australia, Lake Ballard, Menzies, Western Australia
www.menzies.wa.gov.au | www.antonygormley.com

Antony Gormley Australia

Antony Gormley had almost given up hope. But then, while flying across the blue skies of Western Australia, the sculptor spied a vast expanse of white salt, deep into former gold-mining territory. Situated more than seven hundred kilometres east of Perth, Lake Ballard made the perfect blank canvas. Six months later, Gormley stood back to admire his handiwork: 51 figures stepping silently over a seven-kilometre-square patch of the lake.

It's a classic Gormley work. The sculptor is famous for creating human figures to explore identity, the individual, history and context, and this work combines all such themes on an epic scale. Gormley used local residents as models for the figures, while he cast the figures from a specially formulated alloy, made up of elements found among the area's rocks, including iron, nickel, titanium and vanadium. The result is a neat amalgam of man and nature; a hybrid anthropological and geological study as art.

To reach the works, you'll motor along unmade roads through the ghost towns of old gold-mining territory, the detritus of spent industry littered amid the scrub. Arrive at Lake Ballard at midday and you'll witness the figures at their most stark: black silhouettes etched out of pure white under a blistering sun. For the best view, head for a hillock at the west end at dawn or dusk: you'll find the charcoal statues striding in a sea of iridescent purples and pinks. As you walk among the figures, you'll notice that they're curiously reduced forms: Gormley retained the original heights and extremities of his models, but reduced masses and widths by precisely two-thirds, creating concentrated, stripped-down kernels. And as with all Gormley's works, the viewer plays an active role.

The Inside Australia project marked the fiftieth anniversary of the Perth International Arts Festival, held in 2003. It was originally conceived as a temporary work, but interest is so great it looks set to remain, and Gormley may yet install all one hundred works as originally planned. The "ghost town" of Menzies, once at the heart of the gold rush, may yet boom again.

The outback of Western Australia is an isolated territory of billion-year-old rocks, dusty scrub and abandoned mining towns. Thanks to this English sculptor, it's also home to one of the most extraordinary communities on earth.

Above, left and following double page: Most of Gormley's subjects were residents of the nearby town of Menzies and can recognise their own form among the works. If all 100 figures are installed, visitors will have to walk around 42 km to see the whole work.

Helen Martins (1897–1976) transformed her house with Jonas Adams and Piet van der Merwe, while builder and sheepshearer Koos Malgas helped her build the garden.

Helen Martins South Africa

HOW TO GET THERE

The nearest airport is Port Elizabeth, situated around 320 km away. Buses run from the airport to the town of Graaff-Reinet, but you'll need to organise your own transport for the final 50 km leg. You'll find a hire car the best way to explore. Nieu-Bethesda can be found off the N9 towards Middelburg, and the Owl House is well signposted. The hamlet has all the basic amenities including a pub and a coffee shop, good guesthouses and retreats. For a taste of rural Karoo life, try the Doornberg Guest Farm (9 km from the Owl House) which offers horse-riding, game drives and a chance to get involved in farm life (email: peetvh@intekom.co.za). East Cape offers a huge variety of activities and landscapes, from the archaeological sites of the Karoo, and game reserves populated by elephants, mountain zebras lion, cheetah, buffalo and black rhino, to some of the best skiing, surfing and coastlines in the world.
The Owl House, Nieu-Bethesda 6286, East Cape
www.owlhouse.co.za | www.nieubethesda.co.za

Great Karoo is a vast semi-desert plateau found at the foot the Sneeuberg Mountains. Five times the size of Britain, it's a parched land of dolomite spikes, Stone-Age settlements, petroglyths and endless blue skies. Visit the Owl House, planted in a rare verdant valley, and you'll be forgiven for thinking the sun is playing tricks with your mind.

Situated in the hamlet of Nieu-Bethesda, the Owl House is a surreal enclave of rainbow colours and bizarre creatures, created by Helen Martins. The South African grew up here, moved away to teach, and then returned home to nurse her elderly parents after her marriage failed. When her mother and father died she found herself alone, depressed and isolated. What better way to tackle her grief than to transform the family abode?

Martins started on the house in the late 1940s, using luminous paint and coloured glass to exploit the searing light of the plateau. She then used concrete and glass to fashion an exotic coterie of real and mythical creatures, shepherds and wisemen, owls, multi-coloured frescoes, sun-faces and camels. The madcap creations—designed by Martins and crafted by sheepshearer and builder Koos Malgas—reflected her broad interests in Christianity and Eastern philosophy, William Blake and Omar Khayyam.

Martins was keen to be recognised as a serious artist, but locals ridiculed her work. She became increasingly reclusive, and old age, arthritis and failing vision exacerbated her isolation. Having spent 25 years on the project, she tragically took her own life at the age of 78 by swallowing caustic soda.

Martins' Owl House now attracts 13,000 visitors a year, and the hamlet that once dismissed her as a dotty recluse is now a thriving settlement of guesthouses, restaurants, galleries and retreats, making it particularly popular with artists and craftspeople.

Meanwhile, Martins' story endures thanks to leading South African playwright Athol Fugard. Famous for his anti-apartheid stance, the writer based the play the *Road to Mecca* on the story of a rebellious artist grappling with isolation, weaving in an exploration of apartheid, religion, idolatry and the questions thrown up by a notion of a manufactured, personal paradise. Thanks to the play and the Owl House, the legacy of Helen Martins, frustrated artist, lives on.

The doorstep of the Valley of Desolation hardly seems the best address for a depressed divorcee. So how did this location—in South Africa's East Cape—inspire such an outlandish and uplifting project?

Right and following double page: Helen Martins' self-created world include a camel train; sculpted owl figures that serve as tables, bird-baths and even chairs; shepherds and wise men on a pilgrimage. Martin was fascinated by glass-encrusted walls and mirrors that refract coloured light.

Paul Gauguin (1848–1903).

Paul Gauguin Tahiti

HOW TO GET THERE

French Polynesia's only international airport is Faa'a, situated 6.5 km south-west of Tahiti's capital, Papeete. The closest departure airports are in the US or New Zealand. There are 118 islands in total, with Bora Bora and Moorea among the most popular. Diving, surfing, hiking, cruising around the island and enjoying the laidback French/Polynesian culture are popular pursuits. There's a Gauguin museum in Papeari, on the south side of Tahiti. To travel around the island hire a car or flag down *le truck*—Tahiti's public transport system. There are air (www. airtahiti.aero) and ferry connections to many of the islands, including Hiva Oa. The Regent Experience (www.theregentexperience.com) runs luxury cruises throughout French Polynesia, including a jaunt around key Gauguin sites.
Paul Gauguin Museum, PK 51, 2 Papeari, French Polynesia
www.tahiti-tourisme.com

An ex-stockbroker, railing against a soulless material world, seeks a new life. Abandoning his wife and children, he sails 16,000 km to French Polynesia, and spends the rest of his days painting the primitive beauty of paradise islands and their inhabitants.

Paul Gauguin's adventure has such contemporary resonance, it's hard to believe it happened more than a century ago. The French painter first visited Tahiti in 1891, returned to Paris two years later, and then settled on the islands for good from 1895 until his death eight years later. His stay produced some of the greatest works of the Post-Impressionism period: eschewing literal depiction, Gauguin conjured up intense, almost block-carved evocations of semi-clad natives living in a paradise of giant fronds and idyllic beaches.

In truth, Tahiti was not quite the unsullied Elysium perpetuated by Gauguin's paintings and autobiography, *Noa Noa*. When the painter stepped off the boat in the capital of Papeete, he discovered a westernised community steeped in colonial mores. His motives have also been questioned. Far from a quest for an atavistic, noble existence, some claim Gauguin's first trip was in reality a money-making scheme designed to re-invigorate a flagging career: his paintings cleverly evoked erotic fantasies in a style which appealed to European preconceptions of the time.

Whatever you believe, the residency is proof of a life characterised by willfulness and wanderlust. Born in Paris, Gauguin grew up in Peru, travelled the world with the French merchant navy, became a successful stockbroker, worked as a labourer on the Panama Canal and spent time with a half-crazed Van Gogh in the South of France. Meanwhile, he found time to marry and produce five children. The stock-market crash of 1882 proved a pivotal moment, propelling him from amateur to full-time itinerant artist.

Today Tahiti's palm-fringed beaches, blue lagoons and rustic beach huts may be more popular with wealthy sun-seekers rather than impoverished artists, but visit Hiva Oa—a tiny island 1,000 kilometres north-east in the Marquesas—and you'll witness the artist's vision of a simple life. Gauguin lived out his final years on this remote outcrop, penniless and painfully ill with syphilis. The island is a full three hours flight from Tahiti: stop off at his house overlooking the bay in Atuana, and you'll be standing in what is officially the most remote spot in the world.

Keen to escape the pressures of modern life? For a true taste of isolation, take Gauguin's lead and head to the islands of the South Pacific.

Above: Gauguin's grave in the Catholic graveyard on Hiva Oa.
Right: A page from Gauguin's notes, *Noa Noa*.

d'elle en lui, par lui se dégageait, émanait un parfum de beauté qui enivrait mon âme, et où se mêlait comme une forte essence le sentiment de l'amitié produite entre nous par l'attraction mutuelle du simple et du composé.

Était-ce un homme qui marchait là devant moi? — Chez ces peuplades nues, comme chez les animaux, la différence entre les sexes est bien moins évidente que dans nos climats. Nous accentuons la faiblesse de la femme en lui épargnant les fatigues c'est-à-dire les occasions de développement, et nous la modelons d'après un menteur idéal de gracilité. A Tahiti, l'air de la forêt ou de la mer fortifie tous les poumons, élargit toutes les épaules toutes les hanches, et les graviers de la plage ainsi que les rayons du soleil n'épargnent pas plus les femmes que les hommes. Elles font les mêmes travaux

Below: *Where Do We Come From? What Are We?*
Where Are We Going?, 1897.
Right: *The Little Black Pigs*, 1891.

Ingar Dragset (1969–) and Michael Elmgreen (1961–).

HOW TO GET THERE

The nearest international airports are El Paso and Midland/Odessa, 290 km north-west and north-east respectively. Marfa airport, situated around 5 km north of the town, is serviced by a few charter airlines. The area is best explored by car, although you can pick up Greyhound buses from Midland/Odessa to Marfa. Make sure you pack plenty of provisions and take a mobile phone if you are travelling under your own steam. You'll find Prada Marfa on the outskirts of Valentine, a hamlet situated 40 km north west of Marfa on Highway 90. Don't miss Marfa's Chinati Foundation (www.chinati.org), a sculpture park hosting works by Donald Judd, Dan Flavin, Richard Long and Ilya Kabakov. And try to catch the mysterious Marfa lights—bobbing spots of lights believed by some to be the meandering spirit of an Apache chief.
Prada Marfa, Valentine, Texas
www.pradamarfa.com | www.marfatx.com

Elmgreen and Dragset United States

The desert of West Texas is classic cowboy territory: rough patches of acacia and ocotillo stretch as far as the eye can see, while an intense sun bakes saw-tooth mountains and river beds bone-dry. You couldn't be further from 21st-century life. Unless, of course, you stumbled across Prada Marfa—a fashion store sitting amid the scrub.

It's a bizarre sight: a pristine white box situated on the outskirts of Valentine, a hamlet found around 20 minutes' drive from the ranching town of Marfa. Your credit card will stay in its wallet though: despite the alluring lighting, the store's high-class shoes and handbags are not for sale. There's no simpering assistant and the doors are permanently locked.

Known as *Prada Marfa*, the work is the brainchild of Michael Elmgreen and Ingar Dragset, a Berlin-based pair who are in danger of giving modern art a good name. Their works include full-scale replicas of an underground station in New York, a prison cell in São Paulo, and even an entire art gallery in Berlin. The point? Art should be freed from restrictive galleries, they argue, and should land some hefty social, political and economic punches too. So with *Prada Marfa* we have a global brand—built on hallowed western consumerist values of exclusivity and sophistication—

rendered impotent by its setting. Not only are these goods useless in this vast desert, you can't even buy them when you get here.

Prada Marfa is also a neat echo of Elmgreen and Dragset's first major breakthrough. The duo held their first solo exhibition in New York in 2001, trailing the show by placing "Opening Soon Prada" in the gallery window. The bid to send up the gentrification of New York's arty districts actually misfired—some visitors assumed the gallery had closed down—but left the duo with a resolution to use the brand to spectacular effect in the desert.

Surreal boutiques aside, you'll find a trip to West Texas worthwhile. The area has now developed into something of an artists' enclave: Donald Judd's huge sculptures lie just outside Marfa, and the town boasts several galleries filled with work by local artists and artisans. The 1956 classic *Giant* was also filmed here and you can visit the El Paisano Hotel to re-trace the footsteps of James Dean, Rock Hudson and Elizabeth Taylor.

The best experiences are delivered, as you would expect, by nature. The nearby Big Bend National Park offers spectacular hiking right through to the Mexican frontier. You'll need sunscreen, a wide-brimmed hat and stout walking boots—probably not made by Prada.

Former residents of the Rio Grande include native American tribes, Spanish invaders, cattlemen and US troops. Thanks to these artists, it's now home to high fashion.

Right and following double page: Shortly after its opening, vandals broke into Prada Marfa, stole shoes and handbags, and daubed "dum" on its walls. The goods were replaced, but the artists state the store will be "low maintenance" and will deteriorate over time.

Barbara Hepworth (1903–75) in Trewyn Studio Garden, May 15, 1970.

Barbara Hepworth England

HOW TO GET THERE

The nearest airport is Newquay, 35 km and around half-an-hour's drive away. The best way to get there is to take the train: the branch line from nearby St. Erth offers good connections to most major UK cities and drops you right next to the town's Porthminster beach. There are also good coach services to the town, which is around 6 hours' drive from London. You'll find the Barbara Hepworth studio, sculpture garden and museum just a few minutes' walk from the town centre and close to the excellent Tate St Ives, which houses changing exhibitions of modern international and Cornish art and overlooks Porthmeor beach. Do spend some time exploring St Ives' backstreets, away from the pasty, fudge and surf shops, and be prepared for big crowds in the peak summer season.

Barbara Hepworth Museum & Sculpture Garden, Barnoon Hill, St Ives, Cornwall

www.tate.org.uk/stives/hepworth | www.stives-cornwall.co.uk

It's the cusp of World War II, and artist Barbara Hepworth is fleeing London for the country. Accompanied by her husband, British abstract painter Ben Nicholson, she makes a beeline for St Ives—a pretty Cornish seaside resort of cobbled backstreets, sandy beaches, blue seas and, above all, brilliant light. It's a good choice: earlier visitors included Sickert, Whistler and Turner, and the town now boasts a thriving artists' community.

The contours of Cornwall's rolling landscape fuelled Hepworth's abstract style—setting her apart from her contemporary, the more figurative sculptor Henry Moore. But it was the brilliant Cornish sun that inspired Hepworth to elevate capable work into greatness: often satisfied with a piece of work on a grey day, she found herself spurred on to "intensify and release the forms" when forced to reappraise her work under a bright blue sky. "People often think that light is a kind of a chocolate, beautiful and precious thing which one can enjoy", she told the BBC in 1958. "But it's not really that at all. It's a very hard master and teacher."

Pick a sunny day to visit Hepworth's former studio and garden and you'll have an inkling of what she meant. More than 40 of her perforated forms are set in the tranquil garden. The majority cast in bronze—many turning

as green as their setting—they're beautifully crafted, delicate, and strangely life-affirming works. They're also compelling arguments in favour of abstract art: Hepworth may have been inspired by landscape and concrete forms, but she felt the emotions they evoked could only be properly expressed through abstract rather than representational work. For her, a figurative sculpture was a lifeless form. Don't miss the studio either—with hammer and chisels laid out mid-project, as if the sculptor has only just left the space. It's also the spot where Hepworth tragically died in a fire in 1975.

Hepworth and Nicholson's St Ives residency prompted a radical sea-change in British art. The couple were members of the St Ives Society of Artists but a schism between figurative and abstract artists in 1949 prompted them to form the breakaway group, the Penwith Society of Artists. This group in turn spawned a new abstract avant-garde movement counting Terry Frost, Patrick Heron and Peter Lanyon among its members. It's an admirable legacy, worthy of St Ives' brilliant illumination.

The light of this Cornish town has attracted leading artists since the 1880s. Where better for sculptor Barbara Hepworth to develop her radical, abstract style?

Right, top: Tate St Ives overlooks Porthmeor beach.
Right, bottom: Artists were first attracted to St Ives by the availability of low-cost garrets: the former sail lofts of a fishing industry in decline.
Following double page: "Here in St Ives I appreciate every moment of the brilliance and clarity for the forms, for the space that one wants to make within the forms and through the forms." Barbara Hepworth in a BBC interview, 1958.
Left to right: View of Barbara Hepworth Sculpture Garden in spring with Spring (1965) in the foreground.
View of Barbara Hepworth Sculpture Garden in summer with Four Square (Walk Through), (1966).
View of Barbara Hepworth Sculpture Garden in summer.

A snapshot of Ludwig Wittgenstein (1889–1951) during his first journey to Skjolden after the war, in August 1921. It was taken by Arvid Sjörgren, the husband of Clara Salzer, Wittgenstein's niece.

HOW TO GET THERE

The nearest major airport is Sogndal, situated around 1.5 hours' drive from the hut. Sogndal is connected to Bergen and Oslo by plane (www.wideroe.no), and by bus. If you're keen on a more scenic route, pick up an express boat from Bergen to Sogndal (4–5 hours) and take a bus or hire car from there. You'll find what's left of Wittgenstein's cabin situated 3 km away from Skjolden, and a short walk from Vassbakken—home to a campsite and a restaurant/café. The route will take you past waterfalls and into the forest; a signpost and a spray-painted "W" should help direct you. Alternatively, follow in Wittgenstein's wake and take a rowing boat from Skjolden.

Wittgenstein's Cabin Foundations, Lake Eidsvatnet, Near Vassbakken, Sognefjord

www.skjolden.com | www.sognefjord.no | www.wittgenstein-portal.com

Ludwig Wittgenstein Norway

Norway's fjords are a land of plunging glacial valleys and soaring mountains, turquoise lakes, and plateaus of pure ice. Head for the furthest tip of Sognefjord—the country's longest and deepest fjord—and stand on the cliff overlooking the green-blue expanse of Lake Eidsvatnet. Here, you'll witness one man's vision of perfect creative solitude.

An Austrian engineering student who became engrossed in mathematics and logic, Ludwig Wittgenstein started his philosophical studies at the UK's University of Cambridge in 1911. He worked under the tutelage of the brilliant Bertrand Russell, but found fellow academics' displays of intelligence showy. Unable to further his research, he struck upon a solution: complete isolation among the frozen escarpments of Norway.

His tutor tried to dissuade him from going. "I said it would be dark", Russell commented, "and he said he hated daylight. I said it would be lonely, and he said he prostituted his mind talking to intelligent people. I said he was mad, and he said God preserve him from sanity."

The 24-year-old Wittgenstein arrived in Norway in autumn 1913. After spending the winter lodging with the postmaster of Skjolden, he built a simple wooden cabin on the edge of the woods. It couldn't have been harder to reach: the philosopher had to row across the lake and then tackle a steep path to get there. The following spring, the Austrian emerged with the bones of his famously abstruse treatise, *Tractatus Logico-Philosophicus*—an attempt to define the logic of language, and thus, the world. He worked on his theories while serving in the Austrian Army during World War I, and eventually produced a tome that, at least according to its author, solved all the crucial problems of philosophy. As Wittgenstein's only major work to be published in his lifetime, it became one of the most influential philosophical works of the 20th century.

Wittgenstein returned to the hideaway several times throughout his life, and his trips were typically extreme episodes in a tortured existence. He finally returned to Cambridge to teach in 1929, although his career path had oscillated between the highest echelons of academia and jobs as a gardener and primary-school teacher.

As for Wittgenstein's retreat today, Sognefjord may now be known for its physical rather than intellectual pursuits, but it's still possible to visit the site. Only the foundations survive, and you'll get there by foot or rowing boat. The location is a fitting epitaph to Wittgenstein's famous treatise: awe-inspiring, and to most people, utterly inaccessible.

This philosopher sought solitude in the furthest reaches of Iceland, Austria and Ireland, but it took a trip to the fjords of Norway to inspire his greatest work.

Above: A postcard sent by Wittgenstein to his friend William Eccles, another student in Manchester. On it Wittgenstein indicates where he was staying. Right: All that remains of Wittgenstein's house are the foundations on the edge of the woods.

Claude Monet (1840–1926).

Claude Monet France

HOW TO GET THERE

The nearest airport is Paris Charles de Gaulle, 80 km away. Take a train to Vernon, 5 km away on the main Paris-Rouen-Le Havre train line. Fast trains take 45 minutes from Paris, and you can take a taxi or coach, hire a bike and cycle or walk to the house and gardens from the station. If you're driving you'll find Giverny signposted off highway A13 at exits 14 (Bonnières) or 16 (Douains). Parking is free. The only downside is the crowds—some half a million people visit every year. The house and gardens are open from April to October, peak period running from May to June.
Fondation Claude Monet, Rue Claude Monet, 27620 Giverny, Normandy
www.fondation-monet.com

Claude Monet was travelling home to Paris when, glancing out of the train window, he spotted a picturesque village on the banks of the Seine. How much better, he thought, to work here than in the confines of a congested city.

By 1883, Monet was renting a house in Giverny. Buying it seven years later, he embarked on a mammoth 30-year project, cultivating vibrant borders and exotic species, erecting greenhouses and studios, and even diverting the River Epte to create a spectacular water garden. His efforts bordered on the fanatical: when away he left precise instructions for his head gardener, and his correspondence was peppered with anxious enquiries as to his creation's health.

When you visit, you'll see how Monet was cultivating far more than a garden—he was creating an organic muse, and a means to evolve his approach to painting.

During the first few years, Monet drew his inspiration from the surrounding countryside, employing fine brush strokes to depict pastoral scenes. But as his labour of love progressed, he was drawn ever more to the garden, and he started to experiment with colour and new styles. Early Impressionist techniques gave way to broader brush strokes, and he found that he could capture the emotions generated by a scene, rather than the scene itself.

"The subject is of secondary importance to me", Monet commented. "What I want to reproduce is what exists between the subject and me." This subtle evolution produced some of his greatest works, including his haystacks and poplars series and the famous *Décorations des Nymphéas* water lilies.

What didn't change was the painter's routine: Monet used to rise at 5 a.m. and tour the gardens for inspiration. Believing that depictions of nature should be created and reviewed in situ, he painted outdoors and often scrutinised the day's work in the setting Giverny sun, enjoying a well-earned cigarette.

You'll find the property much as it was during Monet's lifetime. The house's colourful interiors, furniture and Japanese prints have been recently restored, while the garden comprises a traditional Normandy *clos*—a walled garden used for growing vegetables and fruit, to which Monet added shrubs and perennials—and a water garden, featuring the artist's famous Japanese bridge and pond, water lilies, wisterias, and weeping willows.

Flowers are planted according to colour, borders are overflowing with trailing nasturtiums, and asymmetry abounds. Visit in the autumn and you'll see a riot of deep blues, reds, pinks and purples; an inexhaustible painter's palette.

The Impressionist artist was famous for his unfettered spirit and love of painting en plein air. This home and garden in northern France proved the perfect retreat.

Right: Admirers of Monet's work and gardens included Matisse, Pissarro, Renoir, Cézanne and Sisley.
Following double page: Monet moved into his Giverny home with Alice Hoschedé, his two sons and her six children. "I was born undisciplinable", Monet admitted. "I equated my college life with that of a prison and I could never resolve to spend my time there, even for four hours a day when the sun was shining bright."

"Hats off, gentlemen, a genius!"
Schumann on Frédéric Chopin (1810–49).

George Sand (1804–76). A hostile reception prompted Sand to brand Valldemossa's inhabitants "barbarians and monkeys" in her novel, *A Winter in Mallorca*, a less than affectionate account of their stay.

Frédéric Chopin Mallorca

HOW TO GET THERE

The nearest airport is Palma de Mallorca, the capital of the island, 18 km away. There is a good network of buses linking the main towns, although you might find hiring a car a more flexible way of exploring the island. The Real Cartuja de Jesús de Nazaret is clearly signposted from the centre of Valldemossa. The town itself is pretty enough, although 'ts pursuit of the tourist euro means chintzy souvenir shops and below-par cafés are now in abundance. Don't miss two other highlights in the monastery complex: a neat garden and a small collection of modern art, including works by Henry Moore, Picasso and Miró. If you're in the UK, you can hear Chopin's work at monthly salon piano recitals hosted by the Chopin Society (www.chopin-society.org.uk). Claustro de la Cartuja, n° 2–3, 07170 Valldemossa, Mallorca www.festivalchopin.com

It's midnight, and the rain is hammering down on the roof of a disused monastery, perched on a hill towards the north-west coast of Mallorca. Inside a damp cell sits a man at a piano, wracked by tuberculosis and half hallucinating. The man is the 28-year-old composer Frédéric Chopin, and he's grappling with a work that is to become his sublime *Opus 28*.

Chopin and his lover, the writer Baroness Dudevant (known as George Sand), moved into Valldemossa's Real Cartuja de Jesús de Nazaret in the winter of 1838. They had high expectations, hoping to escape the French winter and find a refuge where both the composer's health and their relationship could flourish.

But blue Mediterranean skies and the good life eluded them: they were pounded with heavy storms, and their monastery cells were freezing and drafty. The couple also made a poor impression on the locals, hardly helped by Sand's habit of dressing in men's clothing and wandering around the cemetery at midnight puffing on roll-ups. After four gloomy months—Chopin depressed and perilously ill—the couple returned to Paris.

Despite the calamities, the sojourn was far from wasted. Listen to *Opus 28* and you'll understand how such oppressive meteorological and emotional conditions inspired Chopin to write some of his most compelling work, running the gauntlet from stormy torment to melancholy and passion. The composer wrote six of the opus' 24 preludes on the island, and number 4 is worth particular attention; it's thought that Chopin wrote this piece during the midnight tempest, the composer subliminally inspired by the rhythm of the icy drops falling outside. He performed selected pieces from *Opus 28* at Paris' Salle Pleyel on April 26, 1841 to a rapturous reception. The work helped seal the composer's reputation as one of the century's most innovative composers, in turn influencing the likes of Debussy, Tchaikovsky and Rachmaninov.

It's possible to explore the rooms where Chopin and Sand endured their winter. The prime attraction is an excellent series of Chopin recitals every August, and the monastery also houses a small permanent collection of the composer's scores and letters plus his two treasured pianos. But don't expect to find many of the couple's personal effects there—as soon as Chopin and Sand left, the townsfolk burned all their belongings for fear of contracting tuberculosis. Given their fractious relationship, it proved an apt farewell.

This consumptive Pole needed a place to convalesce, compose and spend time with his new lover away from the prying eyes of Paris. A damp corner of Mallorca proved an ill-fated, but productive, retreat.

Left, top: The Real Cartuja de Jesús de Nazaret, as drawn by Sand's nephew.
Left, bottom: A view across to Valldemossa.

Benjamin Britten (1913–76) on Aldeburgh
seafront, 1959.

Benjamin Britten England

HOW TO GET THERE

The nearest major airport is Stansted, situated around 100 km and 1.5 hrs' drive away. There are also frequent trains from London's Liverpool Street station to Ipswich—switch to the Lowestoft branch line and alight at Saxmundham, and take a taxi from there. The Red House is situated near Aldeburgh's golf course off the B1122 to Leiston. There's also a rentable cottage in the grounds. The Aldeburgh Festival is held at nearby Snape Maltings in June, and features a broad programme of new and classical music, opera and visual arts. The venue also runs a year-round programme of concerts and community and education projects. While you're there don't miss the picturesque castle town of Orford to the south, and take time out to explore the wilds of the Suffolk marches.
The Red House, Golf Lane, Aldeburgh, Suffolk
www.brittenpears.org | www.aldeburgh.co.uk

A rare gem on the east Suffolk coast, Aldeburgh possesses nothing of the greasy-chip-wrapper-blowing-in-the-wind desperation that characterises so many English seaside towns. Instead, you'll find a sprinkling of decent restaurants, pubs and galleries, a thriving fishing community, a clean shingle beach and an edifying cultural programme. This rarefied combination is thanks, at least in part, to Benjamin Britten.

Suffolk-born Britten is regarded as one of the UK's greatest composers. A prolific writer by the age of seven, his operas, concertos, symphonies, film scores and choral works are among the most original classical works of the 20th century. Although the composer travelled widely, living in the US and regularly visiting Russia and Japan, it was in this small coastal town that much of the hard graft of composition took place.

Britten lived here for nearly thirty years, moving into a house on the seafront with his partner, the tenor Peter Pears, in 1947. It's an inspiring setting within a pebble's throw of the North Sea, but its exposed position proved problematic—inquisitive passersby used to peer at him working in his study, and on the odd occasion even strolled into the house unannounced. A secluded property, situated near Aldeburgh's

golf course, presented the perfect solution for the couple.

Britten and Pears moved into the Red House in 1957, settling there for the rest of their lives. Visit the rambling 18th-century farmhouse today and you get to see life much as it was during the couple's residency: both an open-doored creative retreat and a domestic hideaway. Portraits, paintings and sculptures fill the rooms—a legacy of the duo's eclectic coterie of writers and artists. As well as providing a retreat for collaboration, the house also provided a good base from which to organise the Aldeburgh Festival, the classical music event that first ran in 1948 and continues today.

Britten's studio was situated in the loft of a barn in the grounds. Accessed by a narrow staircase, it was a spartan affair—a spacious room with large windows, a wooden floor, a grand piano and two large tables. It's here that Britten composed the *War Requiem*, *Death in Venice* and *A Midsummer Night's Dream*, plus numerous orchestral, choral and chamber works.

Before you leave, make sure you take a good look at the front porch on the house's north side: Britten and Pears had it specially built when Queen Elizabeth II visited their abode, en route to opening a new concert hall for the Aldeburgh Festival in 1967.

Living within a few paces of the sea was vital for Benjamin Britten's creativity, but when overzealous fans started to wander into his house uninvited, he had no choice but to find a more private refuge.

Right, top: David Hockney working on a portrait of Peter Pears (1910–86) in the drawing room of the Red House, June 1980.
Right, bottom: "[The Red House is] alas, away from the sea, but thankfully away from the gaping faces, and the irritating publicity of that sea-front. It is a lovely house, with a big garden all round, and I've made myself a nice remote studio where I can bang away to my heart's content." A letter from Britten to Edith Sitwell.
Following double page: Moonlit reeds at Snape Maltings, which hosts the annual Aldeburgh Festival.

William Walton (1902–83) and Susana Walton (1926–).

HOW TO GET THERE

The nearest international airport is Napoli Capodochino, situated just north-west of Naples' city centre. Take a shuttle bus to Beverello port where you'll find regular ferries (1 hour 50 mins) and hydrofoils (50 mins) to Ischia. Minibuses run from Ischia Porto to La Mortella (20 mins). The garden opens from April to October and guided tours are available on request. Try to time your visit to coincide with one of the concerts, held in spring and autumn. The island offers numerous upmarket hotels, but for lower-cost stays try the Poggio del Sole (www.hotelpoggiodelsole.it), a 20-minute walk from La Mortella and a short bus ride from the Negombo hydrothermal park (www.negombo.it). If you find yourself in Naples overnight, the Hostel-Hotel Bella Capri (www.bellacapri.it) offers basic and friendly stays right on the port. The island's southern coast is quieter than the north, so those seeking a *Talented Mr Ripley*-style experience should head to Sant'Angelo or beyond.

Giardini La Mortella, Via Francesco Calise, 39, 80075, Forio (Na), Isola d'Ischia
www.lamortella.it | www.williamwalton.net

William Walton Italy

Ischia is the largest, and some would say most beguiling, island in Italy's Bay of Naples. Volcanic in origin, its wonders include gushing fumaroles and thermal spas, golden beaches and a mountainous interior dotted with pines. Strike north-west towards Monte Zaro, and you'll find an extraordinary garden—conjured magically from a gorge.

William Walton arrived on the island in 1949, accompanied by his new Argentinian bride Susana. The British composer was seeking a place to write his romantic opera *Troilus and Cressida*, and after lodging for several years in an old convent—where the couple endured leaking rooves and rats—they bought a plot of land overlooking the crystal blue seas of the north-west coast. They resolved to make it their permanent home.

It was an attractive proposition for Walton: he found composition extremely stressful, and Ischia presented the perfect opportunity to ameliorate the agonies of writing. Also, after major success in the 1920s and 1930s, some critics were deeming his latest works unfashionable, claiming Benjamin Britten was taking his place as Britain's foremost modern composer. On Ischia he could escape the pressures of London's music scene and leaden skies, and focus exclusively on his work.

While Walton composed, his wife turned her attentions to a garden. Susana Walton started by shipping in tonnes of soil to create a base in a huge volcanic quarry. British landscape gardener Russell Page provided the basic design, and she went on to fill the valley with hundreds of exotic plants, a pool, fountains and cascades, a sun temple and a Thai pavilion. They christened the garden Mortella—Neapolitan dialect for myrtle, a plant that is common to the area.

It's a stunning achievement: well-tended terraces abound with Mediterranean and tropical plants, and you could happily spend a full day exploring the garden's meandering paths. Don't miss the museum, which features a collection of portraits of the composer by photographer Cecil Beaton, and the new Greek theatre, designed by Norman Tree to host concerts by 100-piece symphony orchestras.

One of the best spots to contemplate the composer's legacy is William's Rock, a high outcrop marking the spot where his ashes are buried. The composer drew on a broad array of influences, from jazz to Russian melodies, to write orchestral and choral works, chamber music, opera, ballet and film scores, which ultimately received the establishment approbation they deserved. This spot offers fine views of an inexhaustible source of inspiration—the sparkling Mediterranean.

This Mediterranean island has long exerted a pull over adventurous creatives, drawing the likes of Michelangelo, Henrik Ibsen and W. H. Auden. What better retreat for a composer, grappling with his first opera?

Susana Walton designed the garden to create a place of "harmony and peace" for her husband. She opened the garden to the public in 1991 to showcase Walton's works and establish an education centre for talented young musicians and horticulturalists. It now attracts 60,000 visitors a year. "William said that he wanted this place to survive in time", commented Susana Walton.
Right: The Valley Garden with the main pool and the tree ferns grove.
Following double page, left: The Nymphaeum, designed by Susana Walton as her own memorial, is a surprisingly formal garden among clipped hedges of *Rhamnus alaternus*. The statue of Venus was carved by Simon Verity.
Right: The Thai House, imported from Thailand, is the centrepiece of an oriental garden perched on top of the hill. The Sacred Lotus (*Nelumbo nucifera*) thrives in the pond at its feet.

HOW TO GET THERE

The nearest airport is Salzburg, situated around 50 km south-west of Attersee. From the airport, take the train to Attnang-Puchheim and pick up a bus from there. The lakes are perfect for outward-bound enthusiasts, offering paragliding, scuba diving, waterskiing, sailing, windsurfing, and swimming. For a quieter life, take a steamer across the lake and just enjoy the views.
Attersee, Salzkammergut
www.attersee.at | www.klimt.at

Gustav Klimt (1862–1918): "I am convinced that I am not particularly interesting as a person. There is nothing special about me. I am a painter who paints day after day from morning until night." The artist spent every summer on Attersee from 1900 till his death.

Gustav Klimt Austria

To understand the true meaning of the German word *Sommerfrische*, take a trip to western Austria's lake district. The Salzkammergut boasts picturesque spa towns, soaring mountains and glacial valleys, perfect for hiking in summer and skiing in winter. Spend a few hours on Attersee, the region's largest lake, and you'll see how this aura of "leisurely relaxation" so attracted Gustav Klimt.

The painter spent every summer here from 1900 till his death in 1918, staying in villas on the lake's tranquil banks. Preferring to paint *en plein air*, he could often be seen rowing across the lake's blue-green waters, searching for the perfect scene. Attersee exerted a strong pull over the Viennese intelligentsia, and the painter often found himself in the company of artists, writers, and philosophers, escaping the hurly-burly of city life for a few days of *fin-de-siècle* rumination.

When you visit, you'll find a good Klimt trail gives you an insight into how the painter honed his organic, mosaic style here. He mixed figurative and abstract imagery to produce rich, textured landscapes of the lake and its villas and orchards, drawing on influences as diverse as Van Gogh and Cézanne, Classical Greek, Byzantine, Minoan, Japanese and Egyptian art.

If you can, book yourself into the Villa Paulick guesthouse, situated in Seewalchen on the lake's far north shore. Klimt spent many days here, and it's a prime spot to contemplate the painter's battle-worn life. As one of seven children, Klimt endured an impoverished childhood in Vienna. After art school, he secured a good income through state-sponsored decorative painting, working alongside his brother Ernst and Franz Matsch. But in 1892 his brother died, and artistic differences soon led to a rift with Matsch. A decade later, a high-profile ceiling commission for the University of Vienna attracted accusations of pornography and a fierce row saw the painter hand back his advance.

Such challenging times only served to strengthen Klimt's resolve. In 1897 he founded the new art group, Vienna Secession, which demanded that art be freed from governmental intervention. He went on to reject public patronage, turning to private commissions, and developed a highly ornamental, symbolist style, establishing him as the leading exponent of Viennese Art Nouveau.

Inevitably, controversy was never far away. Klimt broke with the Secessionists in 1905, and his erotic portraits of women prompted further scandal. The peace of Attersee became more attractive than ever.

The academic establishment spurned him, while the state branded his paintings pornographic. No wonder this Viennese painter sought refuge in this stress-free corner of Austria.

Left and following double page: Attersee is a major draw for outward-bound enthusiasts.

The Gershwin art hotel offers affordable stays in New York (far left), while England's Lundy Island makes a perfect writer's retreat (left). Get closer to nature at Costa Rica's School of the World (right).

BOLT HOLES
Canada
British Columbia's Queen Charlotte Islands boast excellent rustic retreats set amid spectacular scenery. Birds, migrating whales, and sea lions are your neighbours, while you can take a break from your masterpiece by walking along the beach, kayaking, or fishing. Try to bag a beachfront cabin if you can.
www.qcinfo.ca

United Kingdom
With no cars, street lights or TV, England's Lundy Island is an unspoilt haven for anyone seeking a few days away from the cut and thrust of modern life. Accommodation options include a lighthouse, castle, fisherman's cottage and campsite, but if it's just you and your muse, try the one-bed Old Light Cottage.
From €196/$236 per week.
www.landmarktrust.org.uk/otherOptions/lundy.htm

South Africa
Stunning waterfalls and forests, and your own cabin with a blazing log fire—what better working environment could there be? The small South African town of Sabie, situated in the Mpumalanga province, also offers spectacular territory for hiking, fishing, riding and white-water rafting. Try the Misty Mountain Chalets for amazing views.
From €37/$45 per night.
www.sabie.co.za/stay/self/SC10/index.html

United States
The best creative retreats combine isolation with natural beauty, and south-east Utah has this in spades. The Arches National Park is a vast expanse of sandstone ridges and mountains, while bike trails and trips on the Colorado River will put some decent thinking space between you and civilization. Hole up in one of Moab Koa's cabins and ponder.
From €36/$44 per night.
www.moabkoa.com

France
Azay-le-Rideau is a fairy-tale village in the Loire valley complete with a Renaissance château, old mill and summer *son et lumière*. Try the Troglododo art hotel, which boasts snug cave rooms rivalling the best Middle-earth fantasy. Productive REM sleep guaranteed.
From €53/$64 per night.
www.troglododo.com

Cuba
For true isolation and low living costs, Isla de la Juventud is hard to beat. Lying off Cuba's south-west coast, this Caribbean hideaway supposedly inspired Robert Louis Stevenson's *Treasure Island*, and offers bags of contemplation-friendly forests and beaches. Don't miss the spooky Prison Presidio Modelo, where Fidel Castro was incarcerated in the 1950s. Find your bolthole among its many *casas particulares*.
www.casaparticulars.com

United Kingdom, Ireland & France
The cliffs of Cornwall or the islands of Scotland? The remote beaches of Ireland's Donegal or the slopes of the French Alps? Welcome Cottages has more than 3,500 villas, apartments, *gîtes* and cottages on its books, many boasting open fires and stunning views.
From €236/$285 per week.
www.welcomecottages.com

India
Arabian Nights fans look no further. Jaisalmer is home to a sandstone 12th-century fort planted in the middle of the Thar Desert. Find a haveli within its walls and get to work. And when the muse deserts you, canter a camel across the sands. Try Hotel Paradise, which boasts a leafy courtyard and good roof terrace (tel: +91 (0)2992 252674).
From €11.30/$1.10 per night.
www.rajasthantravelguide.com/city/jaisalmer.html

CREATIVE COMPANY
Mexico
By rights Isla Mujeres shouldn't exist: just a short boat ride from the package-tour hell of Cancun, this unspoilt tropical island offers lazy days in hammocks, cool beach bars, white-sand beaches and a laid-back Caribbean atmosphere. Head north for the parties and south for creative solitude. Try the Mar y Sol beachfront apartments for longer stays.
From €194/$235 per week.
www.isla-mujeres.net
www.morningsinmexico.com/marysol.htm

Germany
Berlin is now buzzing thanks to places such as Kunsthaus Tacheles. The art space houses galleries, bars and 30 studios—home to creatives hailing from throughout the world. Prospective tenants should send in a CD of their work. If you want to check the place out, stay at the nearby Clubhouse Hostel: at least its all-you-can-eat breakfast will save you from starving for your art.
From €13/$16 per night.
www.clubhouse-berlin.de
http://super.tacheles.de/cms

United States
Moose heads on the walls, artists in residence, fashion shoots and comedy nights—this New York art hotel couldn't be much hipper. You'll find the Gershwin smack in the middle of Manhattan, and a stone's throw from Greenwich Village, Times Square, the Empire State Building and other capital attractions. A cool family suite too.
From €33/$40 per night (dorm beds) and €86/$109 (private rooms).
www.gershwinhotel.com

Slovenia

The capital city of Ljubljana is a green, friendly metropolis, with a decent arts scene and some good bars and cafés. A university population keeps the place young, while its old town, Prague-style architecture and tranquil squares make it perfect *flâneur* territory. Try Stay Ljubljana for self-catering apartments.
From €65/$82 per night.
www.stayljubljana.com

Laos

You could easily crack the best part of a novel in the tranquil city of Luang Prabang, regarded as the seat of Laos culture. This World Heritage site boasts cafés, temples, monasteries and colonial architecture. And after a hard day's creativity, repair to La Résidence Phou Vao, with an infinity pool and inspiring mountain views.
From €121/$147 per night.
www.pansea.com/eng/phou_infor.html

Hungary

Imagine Prague without the crowds. Budapest boasts thermal baths, good museums and galleries, and enough coffee houses to keep you buzzing for a month—the perfect environment to reel off a great work or two. Find yourself your own pad through the Budapest Accommodation Service.
From €40/$48 per night.
www.budapestrooms.com

India

Udaipur is one of the most laid-back cities in northern India, and the perfect place to crack a creative project. Built around Lake Pichola, it's home to palaces and bags of good rooftop restaurants. Find a room in Hotel Mahendra Prakash on the Lake Palace Road—with a swimming pool and Mogul-style rooms—and you may never leave. Tel: + 91 (0)294 2419811.
From €5/$7 per night.

Guatemala

Antigua is a tranquil Unesco town of cobbled streets, laid-back bars, markets and galleries. It's also home to plenty of good hotels—many with courtyards and fountains. For longer stays, try the family-run Casa Ovalle, which offers views of the town's volcano. Email: chataovalle@yahoo.com.
From €191/$235 per week.
www.aroundantigua.com/culture.htm

GUIDANCE AND STIMULATION
Ireland

The Anam Cara Writer's and Artist's Retreat provides space to work on your own projects, and runs workshops covering writing, poetry, painting, drawing and general creativity. The combination of bracing west-coast breakers and country walks should blow away the cobwebs, while you can mull over your work in front of a blazing turf fire.
From €600/$720 per week.
www.anamcararetreat.com

Costa Rica

Fancy brushing up your surfing, Spanish, digital photography, or art skills? This Playa Jacó retreat allows you to pursue all four disciplines. The School of the World is five minutes from Pacific rollers, and well located for hiking, kayaking, and exploring the country's stunning national parks and reserves.
From €412/$495 per week.
www.schooloftheworld.org

Spain

Experienced mentors run residential courses and workshops in creative writing, painting, photography and art at this Alicante mountain retreat. The Old Olive Press is surrounded by limestone mountains, olive groves, and lemon and orange trees, while the beach is just half-an-hour's drive away. Good mountain walking too.
From €632/$760 per week.
www.oldolivepress.com

Australia & Bali

Hone your writing skills and immerse yourself in yoga amid some of the world's most awesome settings. Author and journalist Sarah Armstrong runs workshops and retreats covering both disciplines. Locations include sub-tropical gardens in Byron Bay and the mountains of Bali.
From €115/$140 per course.
www.sarah-armstrong.com

Jean-Michel Cousteau (1938–).

Jean-Michel Cousteau Fiji

HOW TO GET THERE

Fiji's international airport is at Nadi, on the western island of Viti Levu, offering connections to the west coast of the US, New Zealand and Australia. Fiji's Northern Islands are a particular draw for experienced divers, boasting the blanched Great White Wall and Rainbow Reef—a 30-km chain boasting tunnels, ledges and enormous outcrops. You'll find good hiking, fishing, snorkelling and sailing on offer too. To get to Jean-Michel Cousteau's resort you'll need to pick up a connecting flight (1 hr) from Nadi to Savusavu on Vanua Levu.
www.bulafiji.com | www.oceanfutures.org | www.fijiresort.com

On April 22, 1997, thousands of novice divers floated among Fiji's coral reefs, marvelling at their rainbow colours, starfish, sea urchins, moray eels and manta rays. Fortunately their inexperience posed no threat to the fragile habitat: they were exploring the underwater ecosystem from the comfort of their armchairs—courtesy of the world's first live, undersea video chat. The man at the bottom of the South Pacific was Jean-Michel Cousteau, son of famous filmmaker Jacques Cousteau.

Held on Earth Day, the internet broadcast marked a technological, entertainment and ecological first. It was also a symbolic event for the Cousteaus: Jacques died just three months later, aged 87, leaving his son to sweep in a new technologically enhanced era of underwater exploration and campaigning.

Jean-Michel cut his oceanic teeth travelling the world with his parents, producing many of his father's films and television programmes. But in 1992, he broke away from his father's Cousteau Society to set up his own production company, focusing on education programming. He went on to found the Ocean Futures Society, a conservation, research, and education body employing cutting-edge technology to monitor ocean environments. The campaigner also pushed film boundaries by taking part in the 2003 3-D underwater film, *Coral Reef Adventure*. Cousteau has now produced scores of films, employing the latest video, navigation and satellite imagery to create award-winning work.

If virtual exploration doesn't quite satisfy your interest, you should visit the site of that underwater broadcast. Boasting some 330 islands, Fiji is a diving mecca: its reefs are home to the largest variety of coral on the planet, while its waters teem with rays, sharks, turtles, dolphins and more than 1,000 varieties of fish. Inland you'll find tropical forests, geothermal springs and volcanic peaks.

When you visit, you'll notice that Cousteau's activities have extended to that mainstay of eco-conscious tourism—the eco-lodge. His five-star resort sits on a former coconut plantation on the northern island of Vanua Levu. Awash with gushing press reviews, the lodge is proving a major draw for honey-mooning couples, families and, of course, divers. The development was one innovation too far for Cousteau senior though: he objected to the use of the family name in promotional materials and filed a lawsuit against his son, forcing the lodge to include the words "Jean-Michel" wherever the famous surname was used. It seems the handover of a family legacy, no matter how noble the cause, rarely runs smooth.

Son of the pioneering oceanographer Jacques Cousteau, this man virtually has seawater running through his veins. Thanks to modern technology, his family's eco-message is reaching bigger audiences than ever.

Right: At just seven years old Jean-Michel was tipped overboard by his father, the world-famous filmmaker Jacques Cousteau, with one of the first aqualungs strapped to his back.
Above and following double page: Fiji attracts divers the world over.

HOW TO GET THERE

The nearest airport is Heathrow. Most Thames towns are easily accessed by rail or bus. Sonning-on-Thames is situated 30 km from Heathrow and just over 6 km east of Reading; you'll find the Bull Inn—complete with an open fire, exposed beams and small collection of rooms for overnights stays—on the high street. The Thames comprises more than 200 km of non-tidal waters, and you can easily hire a cruiser, canoe or even a Jerome-style rowing boat to explore. Don't miss the nearby picturesque towns of Marlow and Henley, and Hampton Court Palace, royal seat of King Henry VIII. If you'd rather keep your feet on dry land, the Thames Path runs from the Cotswolds to the Thames Barrier in East London offering 290 km of exhilarating walking.

River Thames: Kingston to Oxford
www.visitthames.co.uk
www.waterscape.com/River_Thames
www.jeromekjerome.com/

Jerome Klapka Jerome (1859–1927). The author enjoyed some success with his first two books, *On the Stage—and Off* (1885) and *The Idle Thoughts of an Idle Fellow* (1886) but *Three Men in a Boat* buoyed his finances longer term.

Jerome K. Jerome England

When it comes to instilling a sense of wellbeing, few experiences can match rowing up an English river on a balmy summer's day: willows gently feather the water's edge, swans glide alongside your bows, fluffy clouds float across a perfect blue sky, while a well-tethered bottle of champagne chills in the water. Alternatively, if the writer Jerome K. Jerome is to be believed, such trips are plagued by mercurial weather, food poisoning and recalcitrant hounds.

To find out for yourself, head for the River Thames in south-east England, the setting of Jerome's 1889 classic, *Three Men in a Boat*. The book follows the exploits of three young Edwardian gentlemen, accompanied by their dog, as they take a recuperative break from city life to row east to west from Kingston to Oxford. It's a classic tale, eschewing voguish narrative leaps of fantasy to create humour out of the everyday. Readers are treated to a riot of city-type incompetence amid the great outdoors, ranging from hilarious encounters with belligerent farmers to clueless singalongs in village pubs.

In reality, Jerome started out with serious rather than humorous intentions. Marrying Georgina Stanley Marris in 1888, the couple honeymooned on the Thames and Jerome returned home fired up by the idea of penning a historical guide to the river. Provisionally entitled *The Story of the Thames*, the work was to be broken up by a few comical interludes. "I did not intend to write a funny book, at first", commented the author. "Somehow it would not come. It seemed to be all humorous relief." With the help of his editor, humour took precedence over history, and the writer drew on his numerous river escapades with two close friends, George Wingrave and Carl Hentschel, for extra colour.

Despite the advance of town and tarmac, you'll find scenes that have changed little since Jerome's day: huge swathes of forest still flank stretches of the Thames, while some of its towns remain impossibly picturesque, boasting the olde-worlde charm of cobbled streets and half-timbered buildings. A highlight is the 16th-century Bull Inn in Sonning-on-Thames: Jerome's three roving chaps visit the pub deeming it "a veritable picture of an old country inn".

Three Men in a Boat coincided neatly with the Victorians' love affair with boating, and went on to become a resounding international success. Jerome was catapulted into a successful literary fraternity and his financial worries were assuaged. The book remains in print to this day.

Struggling actor, journalist, playwright and essayist—hard times even forced this man to spend a spell in the doss-houses of London. But could security lie in a guide to the capital's latest craze—boating?

Left and above: Boating on the Thames remains popular to this day.

Jean-Paul Sartre (1905–80) and Simone de Beauvoir (1908–86).

HOW TO GET THERE

The nearest airports are Roissy Charles de Gaulle (23 km north-east of the city) and Orly (14 km south). Both airports offer good shuttle bus and RER train connections to the city's main station, Gard du Nord. From here, pick up line 4 of the Métro, alighting at Saint-Germain-des-Prés. Café de Flore is a short walk from the station. If your pocket can't stretch to the most expensive wine on the menu—the 1860 Petrus 1997 Pomerol—you'll find the £13 Le Flore a good substitute: a coulis of red fruits, Grand Marnier, cognac and champagne. While you're there don't forget to call in at Café de Flore's rival intellectual haunt, Les Deux Magots, situated just over the road. Quieter retreats also abound in the district, including the Jardins du Luxembourg and the city's oldest church, Saint-Germain-des-Prés, founded in the sixth century.
Café de Flore, 172 Boulevard Saint-Germain, 75006 Paris
www.cafe-de-flore.com

Jean-Paul Sartre France

By rights, just walking through the doors of Café de Flore should endow you with artistic greatness. This Parisian institution has played a part in the genesis of surrealism, the French Resistance, New Wave cinema and revolutionary couture. Opening in 1887, its roll call of patrons read like a *Who's Who* of ground-breaking creatives: in the 1930s and 1940s, Simone de Beauvoir, Jean-Paul Sartre and Albert Camus challenged each other in intense philosophical debates within these mirror-covered walls; in the 1950s, Ernest Hemingway and Truman Capote did their best to drink themselves under its tables; and in the 1960s, glamorous fashion designers, directors and actors, including Paco Rabanne, Roman Polanski, Brigitte Bardot and Jean-Luc Godard, could be found hobnobbing under its classic Lalique lighting.

You'll find the café in Paris' Saint-Germain-des-Prés district on the Left Bank, a cultural quarter abutting the Seine and bristling with bars and bistros, galleries, museums, theatres and second-hand bookshops. Although now hugely popular with tourists—it even boasts a shop and its own brand of music CDs—the café manages to retain some credibility as an intellectual hub. An international set of writers, films stars and directors still have their favourite tables, and there's a genuine attempt

to keep its artistic heritage alive with regular play readings and philosophical debates.

To get the most from your visit, take a seat in the quieter upstairs floor and leaf through Sartre's *L'âge de raison* (*The Age of Reason*). The philosopher wrote much of the work here, wrapping up an exposition on free will in a narrative set over two summer days in Paris, 1938. The book tracks a philosophy teacher trying to raise 4,000 francs to pay for an abortion for his mistress, and much of the action takes place in the area's cafés and bars. During the writing, Sartre virtually treated Café de Flore as his home. Accompanied by long-term companion and fellow intellectual Simone de Beauvoir, he used to arrive early to be sure of bagging a seat by a warm stove and wrote and held court here all day.

If you're seeking your own big break, you can bring a play to one of the café's read-throughs. If you're already published, Le Prix de Flore might be of interest. Founded in 1994, the award goes to the writer of the most "original, modern, and youthful" novel of the year; the winner receives a prize of 6,100 euros and a free glass of Pouilly Fumé every day for a year. The award has garnered recognition for several unsung authors but there's one catch—the work has to be in Sartre's mother tongue and published by a French *maison d'édition*.

Pull on the black polo neck, light up a Gauloise and take your trusty notebook to this cafe on Paris' Rive Gauche. If existential inspiration strikes, you could even join the establishment's literati.

Right: Café de Flore yesterday and today. The café has long had a reputation for attracting—and helping launch—relatively unknown creatives, while its rival, Les Deux Magots, has been more popular with established writers and artists.

Samira Makhmalbaf (1980–) (above left) left school at 14 and studied for eight years at her father's Makhmalbaf Film House in Tehran.

Although a popular destination in the 1970s, tourists are currently advised to avoid Afghanistan. However, it's worth noting that Harat—situated close to the Iran–Afghanistan border—is reputed to be the country's safest and most tourist-friendly city. In the meantime, you might want to turn your efforts to helping rebuild a country where the average life expectancy is 43 years old. The Initiative to Educate Afghan Women runs education programmes for Afghan women—denied schooling under the Taliban—while Oxfam is helping build access to services such as health and education. www.ieaw.org | www.oxfam.org.uk www.makhmalbaf.com |

Samira Makhmalbaf   Afghanistan

When Samira Makhmalbaf was photographing women along the Iran–Afghanistan border, she discovered a world of poverty and sickness. Under the very noses of border officials she whisked starving women and children to hospital, saving several lives. It was a typical Makhmalbaf act of munificence meets art.

To read this director's CV, you can't help asking whether you could be doing more with your life. At 18, Makhmalbaf became the youngest filmmaker to compete in the Cannes Film Festival. By 23, she had four films to her name—shooting in Kurdistan, Iran and Afghanistan to explore themes of war, Kurdish oppression and cruel patriarchal regimes. Her work has screened at festivals throughout the world, garnering dozens of awards en route.

Admittedly, filmmaker's genes have helped. Samira's father is Mohsen Makhmalbaf, the famous Iranian writer/director, and her siblings have produced a dizzying array of films, photography and poetry. But since her 2003 release, *At Five in the Afternoon*, the critics have worked themselves into a frenzy over her work: the *New Statesman* rated her as "one of the ten who will change the world", while the UK newspaper *The Guardian* ranked her among the globe's top forty directors.

At Five in the Afternoon depicts Afghan life after the downfall of the Taliban, the story revolving around a Kabul girl dreaming of becoming the republic's first woman president. Brilliantly, it touches upon the burning issues of our times: the chaos of post-war life; the clashes between a dying, oppressive regime, and an emergent, more tolerant culture; the threat posed by extremists, and the redefined role of some women in the Middle East.

Even by this director's standards, the making of *At Five in the Afternoon* was extraordinary. No professional actors were involved—the country's small-scale cinema industry had long since been snuffed out by the Taliban—so Makhmalbaf persuaded numerous locals to take part. She also sourced much of the dialogue from street conversations. The Afghanis were initially suspicious of the project, so the director lived among them to gain their trust.

Sadly, you're unlikely to visit the country's stunning mountains, lakes and ancient cities any time soon. The US-initiated bombing of the country—in response to the Taliban's refusal to hand over Osama Bin Laden—has left a legacy of crumbling infrastructure and civil unrest, while decades of conflict have littered the country with unexploded landmines. We can only marvel that directors such as Makhmalbaf are willing to endure such conditions, and take such risks, for their art.

The pundits claim this prodigious Iranian director will change the world. With her uncompromising depictions of life in the Middle East, they could well be right.

Right and following double page: *At Five in the Afternoon* was an attempt to portray a realistic picture of life in Afghanistan, free from sensationalist war reportage or the rhetoric of "liberating" nations.

Leonardo da Vinci (1452–1519) was the illegitimate son of notary Ser Piero and a peasant girl, Caterina.

Leonardo da Vinci Italy

The nearest airports are Malpensa (50 km from the city) and Linate (7 km). Both are connected to the city centre by bus, with trains also serving Malpensa. Milan's transport hub is its main station, Stazione Centrale, situated just north-east of the city centre. To get to the *Last Supper* and Castello Sforzesco, take the MM2 metro line, alighting at Cadorna. Reservations are essential to view the fresco. The Museo Nazionale della Scienza e della Tecnologia Leonardo da Vinci is a few minutes' walk south of Santa Maria delle Grazie on Via S. Vittore. Milan is a bustling metropolis of bars, cafés, galleries and upmarket fashion stores. The arty district of Brera, to the north of the centre, is particularly worth a visit, boasting La Scala opera house and the city's finest art gallery, Pinacoteca di Brera.

Santa Maria delle Grazie, Piazza Santa Maria delle Grazie 2, Corso Magenta, Milan
www.cenacolovinciano.it | www.museoscienza.org

It started with a simple letter. Aged thirty, Leonardo da Vinci wrote to Lodovico Sforza, the duke of Milan, boasting of his prowess as a military engineer. Warships, cannons, catapults, bridges and armoured vehicles were all within his ken, he promised. And, as something of an afterthought, he added that he could paint and sculpt too.

The letter was a masterstroke of self-promotion. Late 15th-century Milan was a prosperous independent state under constant threat of attack, and military skills were in demand. Leonardo was seconded to the duke's service immediately, leaving Florence in 1482. He stayed in Milan for 17 years.

The duke equipped the young polymath with a studio and a team of apprentices, and gave him free rein. Leonardo was soon exploding contemporary notions of the human anatomy, botany, mathematics, physics, aeronautics and the cosmos. He produced a cache of loose-leaf notebooks—many written in coded mirror text and not properly translated until the 19th century—cramming them with revolutionary drawings and notes on everything from avian skeletal structures to proto-submarines, solar-power systems, hang-gliders and even cars. Few inventions were realised during Leonardo's lifetime.

When you visit, head north-west of the city's gothic Duomo: here you'll find the remains of Castello Sforzesco—the powerbase of Lodovico Sforza's court. The real prize lies just south of the fortress, in the Church of Santa Maria delle Grazie. The *Last Supper* was commissioned by the duke and painted here by Leonardo between 1495 and 1498. Unfortunately, even geniuses get it wrong: the artist favoured oil paints over fresco-friendly watercolours, and just two years after being painted on the refectory wall, the image of Christ and his disciples started to peel.

The *Last Supper* has since suffered trigger-happy Napoleonic soldiers, World War II bombs, the botched handiwork of monks and several attempts at restoration, but its most recent makeover captures the haunting beauty of the original. To see Leonardo's engineering first hand, head down the road to the Museo Nazionale della Scienza e della Tecnologia Leonardo da Vinci, which houses his drawings and models of his machines.

Leonardo's Milan residency cemented his status as Renaissance genius, but he didn't quite live up to the promise of that original letter. The city fell to French troops in 1499, the Sforza family fled, and Leonardo returned to Florence. In hindsight, a pacifist–vegetarian was probably not the best person to take charge of a military infrastructure.

Leonardo da Vinci's grasp of perspective and the human form established him as a leading Florentine artist. So how did his genius come to span anatomy, engineering and the furthest reaches of science?

Above: The Castello Sforzesco, seat of Lodovico Sforza, duke of Milan.

Right: Leonardo's military engineering skills secured his position with the duke of Milan.

HOW TO GET THERE

The nearest airport is Los Angeles International (LAX), 11 km away. Hermosa Beach is situated on the southern side of Santa Monica Bay, ten minutes south of Los Angeles by Metro bus 232 or 439. A taxi from the city will cost around $20. The bay hosts free concerts throughout the summer, arts festivals in May and September, and a good activities such as volleyball, rollerblading and, of course, surfing. Don't miss the Surfer Walk of Fame on the pier, and to check out the surf right now, log on to www.hermosawave.net/webcam

Hermosa Beach, South Bay, California
www.photosgrannis.com | www.hbchamber.net

LeRoy Grannis (1917–). Despite his major success with the camera, Grannis always had to hold down a day job to pay the bills: "I had a family and they liked to eat". He joined Pacific Bell Telephone after serving in the Air Force in World War II, working as a manager until retirement in the 1970s.

LeRoy Grannis   United States

Pick any seminal surfing image from the 1960s and 1970s—from young guns barrelling through enormous Pacific pipes to bronzed longboarders posing on the beach—and the chances are it was taken by LeRoy Grannis. A true surfer's surf photographer, Grannis' genius was born of his participation in the sport—enabling him to capture the machismo and romance of surfing's golden era from an insider's perspective.

Born in Hermosa Beach in southern California—the home of modern surfing— Grannis lived just yards from the ocean and was swimming and bodysurfing by the age of five. He fell in with a close-knit community of surfers and was competing regularly, but it took a stomach ulcer to push him into photography. In 1960, at the age of 42, a doctor advised Grannis to combat work-related stress by taking up a hobby. The camera proved a good choice.

Grannis honed his skills under the tutelage of established surf photographer John Heath "Doc" Ball, and a canny invention helped separate him from the emerging pack of ambitious snappers. In the mid-1960s he designed a small wooden box, sheathed it in plastic and attached it to his board with suckers. The waterproof store contained film, enabling him to keep snapping without returning to shore to re load. The advantage over fellow photographers produced spectacular results, and soon his distinctive super-saturated shots were appearing in leading surf magazines of the day.

Grannis spent the 1960s zipping between California and Hawaii, throwing himself amid thundering mountains of water with abandon. "It wasn't dangerous to me at the time", commented Grannis. "I had a great regard for the water but I wasn't afraid of it." His work saw him inducted into the International Surfing Hall of Fame in 1966.

Tiring of the scrum for the ultimate surf shot, Grannis sought fresh pursuits in the 1970s. Inevitably, they were equally adrenaline-fuelled: he took up hang-gliding photography, until a broken leg in 1981 forced him to switch again, this time to windsurfing.

In contrast to the quiet backwater of Grannis' youth, Hermosa Beach is now a bustling city. However, its beach still boasts golden sands, and the city's surfing legacy is kept alive with the Aloha Days Surf Festival, held every August. Sadly, you're unlikely to witness the photographer hanging ten— now in his late eighties, Grannis hung up his wetsuit just a few years ago after slicing the glassy Californian breakers for more than sixty years.

Ever felt the urge to strike out into a 30-foot swell with a box of film attached to your surfboard? For LeRoy Grannis, such heroics were part of an ordinary day's work.

Left and above: The practice of riding waves dates back hundreds of years among the islanders of Hawaii and Western Polynesia, but the advent of light boards led to a worldwide boom in the 1950s and 1960s.

Below and following double page: Grannis' sealed box of film enabled him to stay in the water for longer, increasing his chances of capturing good shots. He put much of his success down to luck and his decision to chronicling surf culture beyond action shots: "I was just lucky and I photographed more than the surf, but the sidelines too".

Robert Capa (born Endre Friedman; 1913–54). Capa used a 35-mm Leica hand-held camera, which gave him the ability to move quickly on the battlefield.

Robert Capa France

HOW TO GET THERE

The nearest major international airports are Paris' Orly and Charles De Gaulle, around 260 km away. If you're coming by train head for Bayeux, situated 16 km south-east of Omaha Beach, and pick up a bus or taxi for the final leg. The beach is a wild and isolated 10 km stretch of sand so don't expect the usual holiday facilities. The Normandy American Cemetery sits on a cliff overlooking the beach. While you're in the area make sure you visit Bayeux to see the tapestry, a 70-metre-long embroidered depiction of the Norman conquest of England in 1066.
Omaha Beach, Colleville-sur-Mer, Normandy
www.normandy-tourism.org
www.magnumphotos.com

As action heroes go, they don't come much more gung-ho than Robert Capa. The photographer habitually risked his life to capture some of the most disturbing images of war, covering five conflicts with almost suicidal bravado. His good looks, womanising, gambling and fraternisation with the likes of Ingrid Bergman, Ernest Hemingway, Humphrey Bogart and Gary Cooper, all helped secure his reputation as an archetypal alpha male.

Dig beneath the all-American hero persona, however, and you'll find Endre (later Andrei) Friedmann, born of an ordinary Hungarian-Jewish family in Budapest in 1913.

Andrei left home at 18—forced out of Hungary for protesting against fascism—and found a job as a darkroom boy for a Berlin picture agency. Fleeing Hitler's nascent regime, he then decamped to Paris in 1933. The move proved critical: he decided to set up a picture agency comprising three people: Andrei was the darkroom technician, Gerda Taro (in truth, Andrei's Polish fiancée Gerda Pohorylle) was put in charge of sales, while the pictures were taken by an American photographer, Robert Capa.

In reality, Capa didn't exist—all the shots were all taken by Andrei, who favoured the pseudonym for its all-American sound and its similarity to Frank Capra, the famous US film director. The French press were convinced. A

further masterstroke was the pricing of Andrei's work: Capa was so wealthy, the ruse went, that he would accept no less than 150 francs per picture—a good three times the going rate.

Andrei was soon outed but the commercial conceit had served its purpose. The photographer officially adopted the Capa moniker and was eventually posted to Spain to cover the Spanish Civil War, his photograph of a Spanish soldier in the throes of death generating world-wide acclaim. A move to the US and numerous high-profile assignments followed.

For an insight into Capa's extraordinary nerve, visit Omaha beach in Normandy, northern France. Here the 30-year-old photographer, under heavy fire and armed with nothing but his Leica camera, scrambling onto the beach alongside the first wave of American troops on D-Day—June 6, 1944. Capa survived the terrifying hail of bullets, but the nearby American Cemetery throws the horrors of the assault into stark relief—acres of white crosses mark the final resting place of some 9,000 souls.

Inevitably, Capa's luck on the battlefield eventually ran out. He stepped on a landmine on May 25, 1954, while on a *Life* magazine assignment covering the Indochina war. His body was found still holding his camera.

Just how did a Hungarian darkroom boy become the world's most celebrated war photographer?

Left: A view across Normandy's Omaha beach today. Following double page: Capa was the only photographer to pile onto the beach with the first wave of troops on D-Day. He took four rolls of film, but all except eleven frames were ruined in the processing lab.

Paul Bowles Morocco

HOW TO GET THERE

The nearest airport is Ibn Batouta, situated 11 km west and a 20-minute drive from the city. Alternatively, a good way to reach Tangier is to take a boat across the Straits of Gibraltar from Spain—hydrofoils sail from Algeciras (70 mins) and Tarifa (35 mins), while ferries take between 1.5 and 2 hours. You might prefer to follow Bowles' personal itinerary for guests, which focused on the beaches and the Rif Mountains. First-time visitors to Morocco are advised to acclimatise in more tourist-friendly cities such as Fès and Marrakech, although you will find photographs, furniture and other Bowles' memorabilia in the Tangier American Legation Museum in Tangier's medina. Morocco is a Muslim country, so you should dress conservatively—women in particular will attract unwelcome attention if they wear revealing attire.

Paul Bowles Room, Tangier American Legation Museum, 8 zankat America, Tangier 90000
www.paulbowles.org | www.morocco.com | www.legation.org

Perched on the Moroccan coast just 32 kilometres south of Spain, Tangier stands at the very crossroads of Europe and Africa. Its labyrinthine streets are filled with a babble of French, English, Arabic and Spanish; the *djellaba* is a commonplace as western mufti, while the mountains lie kilometres from golden Mediterranean beaches.

It made a stimulating package for the likes of Jack Kerouac, William Burroughs and Joe Orton—not least because living costs were low, a lax liberal regime tolerated homosexuality, while plentiful supplies of hashish fuelled café discussions long into the night. But for some of the best evocations of the area—including its dark underbelly—look to Paul Bowles. The American lived here for more than fifty years, plumbing the depths of Moroccan life in a way that no casual visitor could.

Bowles is as close to a 20th-century renaissance man as you are likely to find. Born in New York, he started out as composer, penning sonatas, chamber works, concertos, ballet and film scores, and as well as incidental music for the theatre. In his thirties he became a music critic for the *New York Herald Tribune*, translated works by Jean-Paul Sartre and Jorge Luis Borges, and wrote a series of short stories.

But in 1947 Bowles's life took a new twist:

he received an advance for his first novel. Bowles had visited Tangier in 1931—sparking excursions through Morocco and Algeria—and so decided to head for the port and set to work. *The Sheltering Sky*—charting the creeping psychological damage of a New York couple as they journeyed through North Africa—was published two years later to critical acclaim, becoming an instant best-seller.

Bowles spent the next half-century immersing himself in the language, fables and music of North Africa, stimulating a flood of productivity. Tangier, the nearby city of Fès and the Sahara Desert became the protagonists in travel pieces, novels and short stories; many dissecting the expat experience with tales of self-destruction, violence and the disintegration of civilisation in hostile climes.

Visit Tangier today and you'll find the laid-back decadence long gone. The port lost its "International Zone" status in 1956, falling under the law of the newly independent Morocco: the brothels closed, nightlife was curtailed and Moorish architecture gave way to unsympathetic concrete. The city still has its fair share of hustlers and seedier corners though, and the qualities that beguiled Bowles are easy to find: the blind alleys of the medina, chaotic souks and more than a hint of danger in the air.

Multi-cultural, laissez-faire and decidedly decadent, Tangier became a magnet for the 20th century's most famous pleasure-seekers. Where better to find material for your first novel?

Left, above and above: Paul Bowles (1910–99) first visited Tangier in 1931. He married playwright and author, Jane Auer; and fraternised with Truman Capote among others.
Right: The cities and landscape of North Africa were often the key "characters" in Bowles' work.

Le Marche's international airport is Ancona, a busy port town which also offers ferry connections to Greece and Croatia. Loreto is situated 27 km south of Ancona, easily accessed by train (20 mins) or bus (just over an hour). Bear in mind that the train station is situated outside Loreto, so you'll need to catch a bus for the final leg. Martin Randall Travel runs all-inclusive Mozart music festivals in Le Marche, featuring performances in several towns including Treia, Tolentino, Fermo and Ascoli Piceno. Spend time exploring nearby Urbino and Macerata, both lively university towns, and the Cónero Riviera, a stunning stretch of white cliffs and coves just south of Ancona. The area is particularly good for hiking and truffle hunting too.

Le Marche
www.mozart2006.net/eng | www.martinrandall.com

Wolfgang Amadeus Mozart (1756–91). Although much has been made of Mozart's hardship, he led a comfortable life by musicians' standards; his periods of penury owed more to volatile relationships with employers and an extravagant lifestyle.

Wolfgang Amadeus Mozart Italy

Wolfgang Amadeus Mozart was just seven years old when he started performing extensively throughout Europe. Under the guidance of his father Leopold, the young keyboardist's virtuosity and improvisation skills—plus his ability to play blindfolded—astounded audiences in Frankfurt, Munich, Vienna, London, Paris, The Hague and Zurich.

Despite this acclaim, Leopold felt his son's extraordinary gifts deserved greater recognition, and so plotted three ambitious tours of Italy. These trips were to be different. On previous excursions, Amadeus' performances had been accompanied by his sister Maria Anna, and their mother had joined the party. But in December 1769, father and son set out alone over the treacherous Brenner Pass from Salzburg to Verona.

Leopold exploited the tours to the full, working hard to ensure influential noblemen witnessed his son's talents. The duo covered a huge amount of ground, travelling relentlessly from Naples and Rome to Florence, Bologna and Milan, with the young genius playing in every concert hall that would host him.

A good place to follow in Mozart's tracks is Le Marche in the north-west, a region protected from the march of modernity by the Apennines to the west, and the Adriatic coast to the east. The teenage musician travelled through the area in 1770, possibly performing at the basilica in Loreto's Piazza della Madonna en route. Despite the development of modern beach resorts and sprawling light industry, you can still find the picturesque hill towns, sandy coves and spectacular cliffs that would have greeted the young musician more than two hundred years ago. It's also one of best places in the world to attend a Mozart concert: due to the region's inaccessible geography, every major town built its own theatre and there are regular performances of the prodigy's work throughout Le Marche.

These Italian tours proved pivotal: during the trips, Mozart was commissioned to compose the opera *Mitridate, Re di Ponto*, had two audiences with Pope Clement XI, and was admitted to the Bologna-based Accademia Filarmonica, a prestigious guild for professional musicians. He also secured his extraordinary reputation for "scoring by ear", transcribing Allegri's *Miserere* from memory, having heard the double choir work just once at the Vatican in Rome.

The international press reported the tours a huge success, and a triumphant Mozart returned home in 1773 to Salzburg, his reputation as one of the world's greatest living musicians secure.

Mozart is regarded as one of the most gifted musicians who ever lived. In truth, it took several years of hard touring to showcase his talents, as these Italian forays prove.

Left: Le Marche is famous for its isolated hill towns, many of which boast their own concert hall.
Above: The basilica in Loreto's Piazza della Madonna, visited by Mozart during his Italian tours.

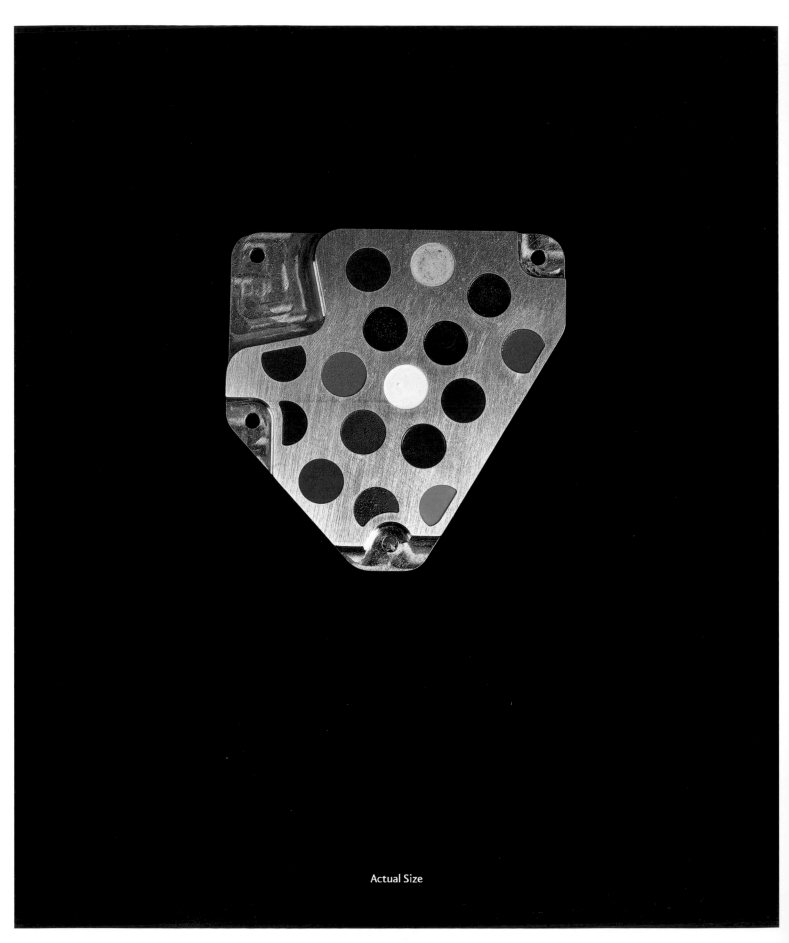

Actual Size

Damien Hirst (1965–): "I'm sure there'll be a great demand for my work out there. They'll love me!"

Damien Hirst Mars

The Virgin Galactic spaceport will be located in New Mexico, near the White Sands Missile Range. The nearest major airport is El Paso, situated 72 km south. First flights are due for lift off in 2008, with seats going for $200,000. You'll need to stump up a $20,000 deposit to secure your place. Although details are sketchy, your fee looks set to buy you full training, negative gravity trips in an executive jet and 0 to 900 kph take-off in less than ten seconds. Alternatively, you could go for the cheaper option and visit the White Sands Missile Range Museum, which traces the history of American space exploration and houses an impressive collection of rockets.

White Sands Missile Range, White Sands, New Mexico 88002
www.beagle2.com | www.wsmr-history.org
www.virgingalactic.com

Combining pluck, eccentricity and no little calamity, there's something quintessentially British about this escapade. A team of British scientists built a probe to search for evidence of life on Mars, and needed a way to calibrate its colour sensors once it thumped down into the red dust. Damien Hirst, erstwhile *enfant terrible* of British art, was only too happy to oblige.

Alongside sharks preserved in formaldehyde and cows sawn in half, spot paintings are among Hirst's most famous works. The artist has covered walls and massive canvases with symmetrically placed spots of every imaginable hue. What better way to combine science and art then, than by attaching a spot painting to a Martian probe? The work would fulfill a key scientific need—enabling sensors to accurately analyse the colours of Martian soil—and would be a boon for the art world, becoming the first work exhibited on another planet.

Hirst created a bespoke spot work, which was duly attached to the $79-million Beagle 2 lander. A composition by the British pop band Blur—to be broadcast upon touchdown— was added to the creative cargo, and the ensemble blasted off from Kazakhstan's Baikonur space centre in June 2003 aboard the European Space Agency's Mars Express spacecraft. The combination of pioneering scientific endeavour

and quirky British ambition generated huge public attention—ranging from keen support to calls to jettison the artists themselves into outer space.

But on December 25, 2003, after Beagle 2 had separated from its mother ship and was floating down through the thin Martian atmosphere, something went wrong. Although slowed by parachutes and cushioned by airbags, it's thought that the probe hit the surface too hard and may have disappeared into a crater. There was no triumphant broadcast of Blur's tune and the probe failed to transmit a squeak of data back to earth. We can assume that Hirst's work was installed though, possibly in several pieces.

It will be a while before you can view Hirst's work in situ, but space travel is far from light years away. Those with deep pockets can follow the world's first space tourist, Dennis Tito. The millionaire businessmen blasted off from Kazakhstan in 2001 and spent eight days on the International Space Station, paying $20 million for the privilege. Those on more limited budgets should head for a Richard Branson's Virgin Galactic spaceport in New Mexico, which aims to run sub-orbital trips by 2008.

This work whizzed millions of kilometres through the cosmos, and battled through fierce dust storms to reach its final exhibition space. There may not be life, but there almost certainly is art, on Mars.

Left: Damien Hirst, *Mars (Beagle 2)*, 2002. Aluminium and pigment paint.
Above: New Mexico's White Sands Missile Range presents a comprehensive history of American space exploration. Following double page: Beagle 2 was due to touch down on Mars on December 25, 2003. Analysis of the landing site suggests it may have fallen into a crater. The expedition was designed to detect present or past life on Mars.

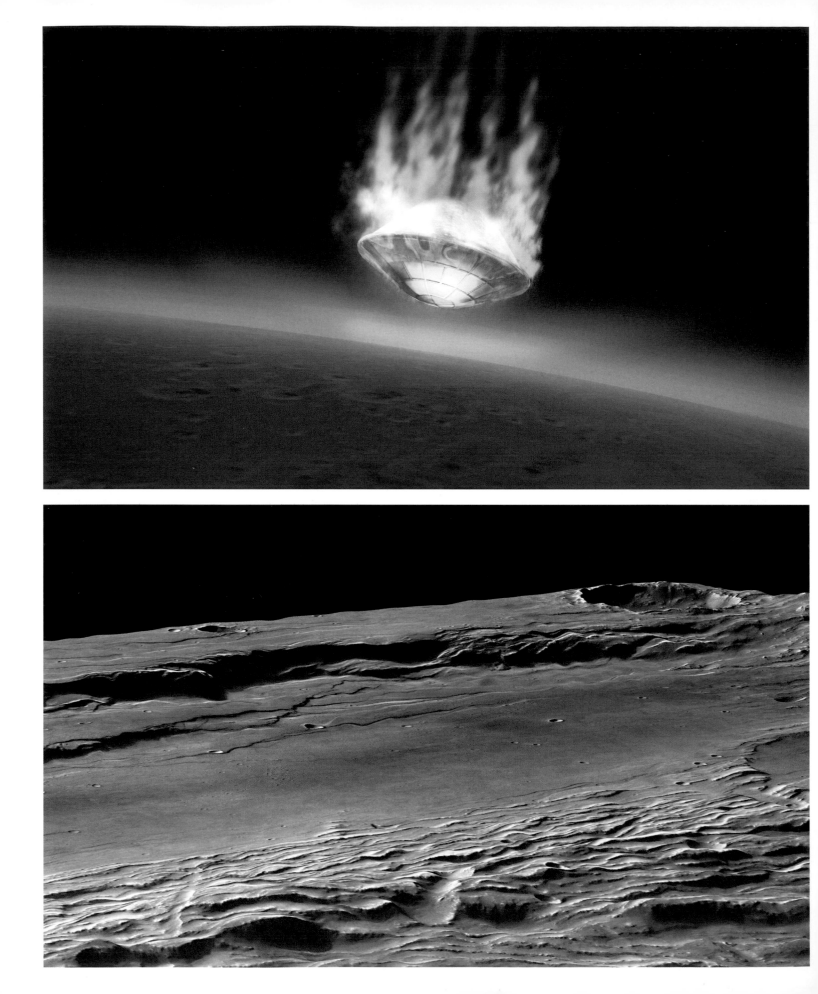

New York's Mercer Hotel (left and centre right) and Beijing's Red Capital Club (far left) are a magnet for movers and shakers, while Hidden Art (right) supports designers.

CHANCE ENCOUNTERS
United States
If you're keen on bumping into media moguls or Hollywood stars over breakfast, New York's Mercer hotel is a pretty good place to start. Awash with designer features, from flat-screen TVs to exposed brick interiors, this SoHo haven attracts the likes of Quentin Tarantino, Russell Crowe and Calvin Klein.
From €360/$440 per night.
www.mercerhotel.com

China
The world's fastest-growing economy is generating its fair share of millionaires just itching to invest in creative projects. The question is, where to track them down? Bejing's Red Capital Club restaurant is a good place to start: its 1950s-style revolutionary-era interior proving a magnet for thrusting young capitalists. A good boutique hotel too.
From €25/$31 per person.
http://redcapitalclub.com.cn

Italy
If Sartre and Camus were alive today, they'd be battling over the finer points of existentialism here. Le Trottoir is packed to the gills with an intellectual and creative set, and sits handily on the doorstep of the city's arty Brera district. The bar also hosts a busy programme of film screenings, live music, exhibitions and theatre.
www.letrottoir.it

Greece
Bar a fountain spouting free money, this Athens bar boasts everything a budding artist could want: live tunes, heart-warming comestibles and libation, some decent exhibitions and a good vibe. Stavlos, found in the Thisio district, is also a mecca for local arty types, so the chances are you'll agree to at least one loony collaboration while propping up the bar.
www.stavlos.gr

United States
Keen to hobnob with the hipsters but have kids in tow? This baby-friendly New York tea lounge might well provide the answer. Situated on Brooklyn's Park Slope, its velvet window seats and mismatched sofas accommodate a go-getting yet chilled crowd. An admirable array of fresh brews on offer too.
www.tealoungeny.com

Brazil
A long-established mecca for beautiful people wearing precious little, Rio de Janeiro's Ipanema Beach is now a magnet for trendsetting movers and shakers, particularly during the weekend pose-athon. And beyond the white sand and dental-floss G-strings you'll find bags of cool bars. Where better to clinch that deal?
www.ipanema.com

Ibiza
Situated at the very southern tip of the island, Las Salinas beach is where you'll find the rich, talented and drop-dead beautiful. For something a tad more bohemian, head north for the sheltered bay of Benirras, where musicians bring out the guitars and drums for sundown jams.
www.ibiza-spotlight.com

Switzerland
Your novel is a best-seller, while you've been told to clear a space on your mantelpiece for the Nobel Prize for Literature. Well, every artist can dream, and where better to drift off than at Seebad Enge—a bathing pavilion built over a lake in Zurich, and a surefire hangout for designers and filmmakers.
From €4/$5 per person
www.tonttu.ch

SHOWCASE YOUR WORK
London
Jimi Hendrix and Bob Dylan blew away audiences at the Troubadour, and decades later it still ranks as one of London's finest venues. This arty establishment is constantly on the lookout for unsigned musical talent, so send a CD of your work, and you could be taking to the stage quicker than you can say "25 bottles of JD on the rider". Poetry, screenings and exhibitions on offer too.
www.troubadour.co.uk

United States
Held in New York in June, the Affordable Art Fair is where you'll find the great artists of the future. Work includes painting, photography, drawing, sculpture and video, and prices range from $100 to $5,000. To exhibit you do need to be on the books of a gallery.
€10/$12 per ticket
www.aafnyc.com

France
Thanks to a year-round festival programme, Toulouse is one of Europe's most invigorating cultural hubs. The autumn Printemps de Septembre is the one to go for: an international riot of jazz, painting, photography, video, cinema and performance. Contact the festival office to be part of the show.
www.printempsdeseptembre.com

Cambodia
This Phnom Penh art foundation hosts exhibitions, screenings and theatre from all over the world, as well as showing the best of local talent. The Java Café and Gallery is where the glitterati hang out; the coffee isn't bad either.
www.javaarts.org

China

Situated in Bejing's Dashanzi district, this old Soviet-era factory is now chock full of up-and-coming galleries, studios, designers, architects, sculptors and bars. Dubbed 798, it regularly hosts cutting-edge exhibitions, concerts and bizarre performance art. Get your show in quick before the developers start revving the bulldozers.
www.798space.com

Brazil

Whether you're a contemporary artist, architect, fashion designer, filmmaker or technology nut, São Paulo is one of the best places on the planet to showcase your work. The International Art Biennale is a monster, running for three months (dates vary). Just take a deep breath and plunge in.
www.brazilmax.com
www.bienalsaopaulo.org.br

Mexico

The picturesque town of San Miguel de Allende boasts a thriving artist colony, numerous galleries and the famous Bellas Artes Institute. Mix with fellow artists, take classes in anything from painting and sculpture to collage and ballet, and take advantage of the town's legendary light. Try Casita de Las Flores for good value self-catering stays.
From €20/$25 per night;
€360/$460 per month.
www.sanmiguelartists.com
www.casitadelasflores.com

Iceland

Reykjavik, Europe's northernmost capital, hosts nearly two dozen arts festivals a year and bristles with bars and avant-garde performance spaces. And when the pressure gets too much, head out of town for the geothermal pools, glaciers, hot springs and volcanoes. Your first stop should be the ultra-hip 101 Hotel and adjoining gallery.
From €295/$359 per night.
www.visitreykjavik.is

A HELPING HAND
Worldwide

With art galleries taking hefty slices of a work's sale price, cutting out the middle-man has never looked to attractive. Tap into a global fraternity of buyers by uploading your work for free to this website, set up by art dealer Charles Saatchi. Best of all you pay zero commission.
www.saatchigallery.com/yourgallery

United Kingdom

Film London supports new filmmakers based in the capital through grants, courses, competitions and festivals. Genres include shorts, feature films, animations and contemporary art. Its movie maps allow you to indulge in Britflick fantasies too, charting locations used for *Love Actually*, *Bridget Jones's Diary* and *Closer*.
www.filmlondon.org.uk

Worldwide

Hidden Art is a not-for-profit organisation that helps designers sell their work. Membership gives you the chance to exhibit at international design fairs, plus provides access to networking sessions, training and advice. It's based in London and has a network of members, suppliers, manufacturers and buyers worldwide.
Membership: free to €146/$186 per year.
www.hiddenart.com

Worldwide

Got a hot screenplay idea you're trying to turn into reality? The Scriptfactory offers support services including training, script feedback masterclasses and performed readings. It runs sessions around the world, including in Brazil, Israel, Singapore, Poland, Australia and the UK. Email newsletter free.
Membership: €58/$70 annual fee.
www.scriptfactory.co.uk

Although his identity is a closely guarded secret, Banksy is thought to be from Bristol in the UK. His real name is reputedly Robin Banks, but the obvious joke makes this unlikely.

Banksy Israel/West Bank

HOW TO GET THERE

The nearest airport is Ben Gurion Airport, situated 50 km west of Jerusalem and connected to the city by regular buses and taxis. It is possible to see Banksy's murals but be aware that you are entering a potentially volatile zone. The easiest one to visit is Banksy's painted ladder at Abu Dis. Meanwhile the Kalandia checkpoint is situated 16 km (around 20 minutes' drive) north of Jerusalem. Whichever work you visit go with an organised group or with an Arab taxi driver in a party of at least two. Be aware that you will be questioned by the Israeli army. The West Bank is home to a wealth of historical and archaeological riches, including the ancient settlements of Jericho, Bethlehem and Nablus—religious sites that are significant to Muslims, Jews and Christians. For guided tours, try the Jerusalem Hotel or the Palestinian Association For Cultural Exchange (PACE). Kalandia checkpoint, Abu Dis, Bethlehem, West Bank
www.pace.ps | www.banksy.co.uk
www.jrshotel.com/jrshotel-old/tours/index.html

Banksy is a globetrotting guerrilla artist who appears to know no fear. The Brit has struck in Melbourne, London, Spain and San Francisco—and in many places in between—daubing his work on elephant enclosures, trains, ships and even the flanks of live animals. His efforts include witty incitements to riot, giant rats, fallen angels and bogus cashpoints spewing fake money—speedily stencil-sprayed for accuracy.

To see how far Banksy is willing to go for his art, take a look at his handiwork on the eight-metre-high wall slicing through the West Bank between Israel and the Palestinian Territories. The concrete structure is part of the "Separation Barrier", which comprises a planned 800 kilometres of "security" wall, fence and ditch being built by the Israeli government, which claims it is needed to deter suicide bombers. Much of the barrier's trajectory is in breach of international law, and it has been heavily criticised for cutting into Palestinian land, barricading settlements and appropriating farmland and water supplies.

Banksy visited the barrier in 2003. Under watchtowers manned by Israeli soldiers, he proceeded to paint bucolic "views" through illusory cracks in the wall. A boy appeared on a sandcastle near the Kalandia checkpoint, a snow-capped mountain was magicked up at the Bethlehem crossing, while a small boy appeared by a rope ladder snaking to the top of the barrier at Abu Dis. The painting sessions were hardly stress-free: guns were fired in the air while Banksy worked. "Palestine is now the world's largest open-air prison", concluded Banksy, who escaped unscathed, "and the ultimate activity holiday destination for graffiti artists".

Although not in the same death-defying league, Banksy's high jinks have since extended to art galleries. In London he sneaked a rat sporting sunglasses and a rucksack into the Natural History Museum; in New York he installed a gasmask-adorned portrait in the Metropolitan Museum of Art as an anti-war ruse; and visitors to Paris' Louvre were alarmed to find the *Mona Lisa*'s enigmatic smile had been replaced by an Acid House smiley face.

The artist's efforts are so laden with social comment and wry observational humour, that to dismiss Banksy as a vandal or art terrorist is to do him an injustice. "The people who truly deface our neighbourhoods are companies that scrawl their giant slogans across buildings and buses", insists Banksy, "trying to make us feel inadequate unless we buy their stuff". Thankfully, reported commissions from Nike have been turned down, while the artist's identity is still a closely guarded secret.

Daubing your work under the glare of streetlights or closed-circuit television is one thing. But how steady would your hand be under the sights of loaded rifles?

Right: Banksy's efforts at the Kalandia checkpoint. Following double page: The Separation Wall runs in sections throughout the Occupied Territories. Its planned total length is 800 km.

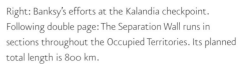

Jackson Pollock (1912–56). "There's me and there's Picasso. The rest of you are whores!" Pollock's reputed rant at a local bar while living on Long Island. Sally Vincent, *The Guardian*, 1999.

Jackson Pollock United States

HOW TO GET THERE

The nearest airport is Islip/MacArthur, situated just over 100 km from the house. Pick up Hampton Jitney coach service (www.hamptonjitney.com) or the train (http://mta.nyc.us/lirr) to East Hampton (around 1.25 hours). Both services start in New York City. You'll have to take a taxi for the final leg to the house, situated 6.5 km north of East Hampton. The house and studio are open to the public from May to October. The Hamptons is an upmarket enclave at the far eastern end of Long Island, situated around 160 km east of New York. For a place to stay, try the East Hampton Chamber of Commerce (www.easthamptonchamber.com) but be prepared to dig deep. Pollock-Krasner House and Studio, 830 Fireplace Road, East Hampton, NY www.pkhouse.org

As hell-raising artists go, it's difficult to imagine someone more iconic than Jackson Pollock. The Abstract Expressionist painter was a chronic alcoholic and a depressive. His mental breakdowns, bouts of self-doubt and self-destructive fury provided a disturbing backdrop to his art—which ranged from surreal and symbolic to frenetic and chaotic.

For an insight into Pollock's life and art, head for The Springs, a hamlet in East Hampton on Long Island, in the US. The painter moved here from New York in November 1945 with his wife, the artist Lee Krasner, using a loan from Peggy Guggenheim as down-payment on a fisherman's house and barn. It's an idyllic spot overlooking the tranquil backwater of Accabonac Creek.

You'll still find much of the couple's domestic flotsam and jetsam intact, including their jazz records and library. The highpoint is undoubtedly the barn studio. Once you've donned a pair of protective slippers, you can pad around the paint-splattered floor where Pollock developed his groundbreaking "action painting" technique. Dispensing with an easel and brush, Pollock used to lay a canvas on the floor and almost physically assault it, pouring, splashing, squeezing and flinging paint onto its surface, while throwing cigarette butts, broken glass and sand into the mix.

Pollock likened the approach to American Indian sand painting—circling the canvas to be physically "in the painting". But whereas Navajo shamans employed precise strokes to depict spiritual imagery, Pollock used spontaneous acts to express raw emotion. Interestingly, this primal process was developed during a period of complete sobriety, between 1948 and 1950. The demons channelled, it became one of the most productive spells of Pollock's life. The action paintings were a triumph, prompting Life magazine to run the rhetorical headline: "Jackson Pollock: Is he the greatest living painter in the United States?"

Sadly, the glory days couldn't last. By 1951 Pollock's style had shifted once more: monochrome replaced colour and figurative imagery crept in. The reception was lukewarm. By 1955 Pollock's mental and physical health was deteriorating fast: he was unable to handle the pressures of fame and his drinking was so out of control that he couldn't work at all. Their marriage under strain, Krasner visited Europe to reassess their relationship. She took a telephone call on August 12, 1956, informing her of her husband's untimely, but most would say inevitable, demise. The painter had died in a car crash, killing himself and his mistress while drunk at the wheel. He was 44 years old.

Fame and financial success failed to save Jackson Pollock from his personal demons. But if he had not moved to The Springs, a hamlet on Long Island, his radical "action paintings" may never have been born.

Above: The artist moved to this fisherman's house in East Hampton in 1945.
Right: Jackson Pollock was dubbed "Jack the Dripper" by *Time* magazine in 1956.

Aleister Crowley (1875–1947) (second left) with fellow mountaineers during a 1902 expedition.

HOW TO GET THERE

The nearest international airports are in Bagdogra, situated 74 km away in Darjeeling, India and Kathmandu's Tribhuvan International (50 km away). You'll find Kanchenjunga in the far east of Nepal, on the border with Sikkim, a former Himalyan kingdom that is now part of India. You'll need to pick up a connecting flight to the small airstrip of Taplejung to get closer to the mountain. Kanchenjunga can only be attempted by very experienced climbers, although there are shorter guided treks from both north and south base camps. Eco Trek International runs treks to Kanchenjunga's south base camp and across to its northern side.

Sukhetar and Ramche (base camps), Kanchenjunga
www.nepaltourism.info | www.ecotour.com.np

Aleister Crowley   Nepal

In August 1905, a team of mountaineers left Darjeeling for the treacherous peaks of East Nepal. Their target: the unconquered summit of Kanchenjunga—the third highest mountain in the world. Their leader was the notorious mystic, Aleister Crowley.

Crowley led his team up Kanchenjunga's icy escarpments with gusto, brushing off the effects of altitude sickness while remaining, according to his memoirs, "fresh as paint and as fit as a fiddle". But on the final leg, a good three-quarters of the way towards the 8,600-metre summit, six men turned back and triggered a huge avalanche. Despite hearing their cries for help, Crowley bedded down for the night. When he descended the next day, he found four men crushed to death.

Crowley's mountaineering career was at an end, and an ensuing penchant for sex, "magick" rituals, opiates and animal sacrifices—plus a fondness for the monikers "the beast" and "666"—made him an obvious target for vilification by the British media.

The ill-fated climb was entirely in keeping with Crowley's bizarre life. Aged just 29, his feats included a world survival record of 65 days on a glacier, an unfinished Cambridge University degree, immersion in yoga and Buddhism, an aborted attempt to scale Chogo Ri (K2), and a disruptive stint with the occult

group The Hermetic Order of the Golden Dawn. Crowley had also just declared himself a prophet of a new world order based on individual freedom, known as Thelema. All these escapades were bankrolled by a fortune inherited from his father's brewing empire.

To re-live that fateful climb, dip into the occultist's autobiography, *The Confessions of Aleister Crowley*. It's a masterpiece of bravura: a mixture of travelogue and mystic exegesis, told with bellowing self-belief. Unsurprisingly, the work absolves Crowley of all blame for the accident: he had warned the "mutineers" that they would die if they tried to descend, he claims, and nightfall prevented him from coming to their aid any earlier. It seems Crowley saw the expedition as opportunity to pit his personal will against the forces of nature. "I was very sad at heart about the death of my friends", he noted, "but with regard to the mountain I was in excellent spirits".

Today, Kanchenjunga is regarded as an even harder climb than Everest. Its avalanches are said to be the world's fiercest, while a paucity of tourists, established trails and fixed lines makes an ascent particularly challenging. Those wishing to avoid Crowley-style endurance tests should stick to the lowlands of Darjeeling or the alpine meadows, Buddhist temples and wildlife sanctuaries of Nepal.

Occultist, poet and fearless mountaineer: Aleister Crowley was one of the 20th century's most controversial figures. This trek gave the press another reason to label him the "wickedest man on earth".

Right: Nepal is famous for its tea plantations and hillside villages.

Following double page: Crowley's men made it three-quarters of the way up Kanchenjunga before a tragic accident put paid to the attempt.

Written After Swimming from Sestos to Abydos

If, in the month of dark December,
Leander, who was nightly wont
(What maid will not the tale remember?)
To cross thy stream, broad Hellespont!

If, when the wintry tempest roared,
He sped to Hero, nothing loath,
And thus of old thy current poured,
Fair Venus! how I pity both!

For me, degenerate modern wretch,
Though in the genial month of May,
My dripping limbs I faintly stretch,
And think I've done a feat today.

But since he crossed the rapid tide,
According to the doubtful story,
To woo—and—Lord knows what beside,
And swam for Love, as I for Glory;

'Twere hard to say who fared the best:
Sad mortals! thus the gods still plague you!
He lost his labour, I my jest;
For he was drowned, and I've the ague.

HOW TO GET THERE

The nearest airports are Atatürk International, situated 317 km north-west in Istanbul, and Izmir, 340 km south. From either airport, head for the coach terminal and pick up an intercity bus to the town of Çanakkale (around five hours). Abydos lies around 5 km from here and is marked, as is Sestus, by an ancient castle. Be aware that Abydos is now a military zone, so the only way to get there is by boat, and you need a permit to land there. The strait is now a busy shipping lane, but if you are feeling particularly adventurous contact Swimtrek: the company runs organized trips for strong swimmers and provides escort boats. The area is also famous for its golden beaches and ancient sites, as well as the battlefields, cemeteries and memorials of the 1915 Gallipoli campaign.

Abydos, Çanakkale, Dardanelles, Turkey
www.internationalbyronsociety.org
www.swimtrek.com/helles_pont.htm

"I plume myself on this achievement more than I could possibly do on any kind of glory, political, poetical or rhetorical." Lord Byron (1788–1824), on having successfully swum the Hellespont, from Europe to Asia, in 1810.

Lord Byron Europe/Asia

It was never going to be a conventional trip. George Gordon Noel Byron, accompanied by a trusty valet and an old school friend, set sail for Portugal from England on July 2, 1809. Upon their arrival in Lisbon, the trio rode over six hundred kilometres to Seville and Cadiz, sailed on to Gibraltar, Sardinia and Malta, and then toured overland through Albania, Greece and Turkey.

Throughout the two-year journey Byron threw himself into heroic feats of athleticism, seduction and over-indulgence with gusto. The louche baronet swam Lisbon's Tagus river, conducted affairs with women and boys, partied hard in Athens and was wooed by an Albanian tyrant. The trip was edifying too—taking in the ancient sites of Sunium, Attica and Marathon—and left the poet with two unwelcome souvenirs: malaria and gonorrhoea.

A heavily embroidered version of this caper is captured in Byron's epic travelogue, cantos I and II of *Childe Harold's Pilgrimage*. Written while on the road, it's a thumping work of self-aggrandisement, introducing the world to an aristocratic aesthete, vagabond and feckless Romantic. The work was published in 1812 to great commercial success, and Byron "awoke and found himself famous".

To experience something of these high jinks, head for Dardanelles (formerly Hellespont) in north-west Turkey. The strait separates Europe and Asia, and strong currents flow here between the Aegean and the Black Sea. Byron stopped off at its narrowest point on the trail of a famous Greek myth. The young lover Leander, the legend goes, swam nightly across the river from Sestos to Abydos to reach Hero, a priestess of Aphrodite, guided across the water by her lantern. One night the light was extinguished by the wind, and the young lover died. Devastated, Hero committed suicide.

When Byron arrived here in 1810, he couldn't help himself: a strong swimmer, he dived in and battled across the strait, powering through three kilometres of choppy currents in homage to the myth. He reached the other side, triumphant. If you time your visit well you can pay homage to the poet's aquatic adventure: there are guided swims across the strait in the summer. Or if you prefer to keep your feet on dry land, you should head for the site of another Greek myth—the nearby ancient city of Troy.

When the 21-year-old Lord Byron was plotting his Grand Tour, the Napoleonic Wars had put the traditional route through France and Italy out of bounds. An alternative trail gave the poet more than enough to write home about.

Above: Strong swimmers can still conquer the 3-km channel from Abydos to Sestos, on organised trips. Depending on tides and the weather, it usually takes between one and two hours.

Ernest Hemingway (1899–1961) wrote both at Harry's Bar and the Locanda Cipriani hotel in Venice, travelling between the two by boat.

The nearest airports are Treviso, 30 km inland, and Marco Polo, 7 km north of the city. Both offer connections to the city centre. Arriving by car is not recommended. You'll find Harry's Bar in the San Marco district, towards the south of the city. Despite hordes of visitors, particularly during the peak summer season, Venice is still a must-see destination, particularly as rising sea levels are threatening its existence. Walking aimlessly is pleasure enough: Venice boasts some 150 canals and at least 400 bridges and is best navigated by foot or by waterbus (vaporetti and the smaller motoscafi). While you're there don't miss the Basilica di San Marco, the final resting place of the city's patron saint, and the Tintoretto at the Scuola di San Rocco. Be aware that prices for food and accommodation are high, but if you have the funds the legendary gondolas are worth every euro.

Harry's Bar, San Marco, Calle Vallaresso, 1323 Venice
www.cipriani.com

Ernest Hemingway   Italy

When Ernest Hemingway holed up in the world's most romantic city to write a novel, it's easy to see why he gravitated towards Harry's Bar. Set in an idyllic spot on St. Mark's bay waterfront, this establishment was the very embodiment of Italian chic. Tuxedoed waiters mixed stiff bellinis and whisky sours at a chrome-topped bar, while frosted glass kept prying eyes from the likes of Orson Welles, Charlie Chaplin and Truman Capote.

The Harry's Bar formula has now spread to London, New York and Hong Kong but the Venetian original definitely warrants a visit, if only to picture Hemingway at his favourite corner table, regaling friends with embroidered tales of drinking, boxing and hunting. Push open the understated Art Deco door and you'll find little has changed since the writer's day: smart locals crowd the over-lit, snug interior, while a plate of carpaccio and a few rounds of cocktails will still eat up the best part of a week's salary.

Hemingway arrived in Venice in the autumn of 1948 to write *Across the River and Into the Trees*, penning several pages on this establishment's walnut tables. His regime was surprisingly disciplined: after spending the evening at the bar he usually repaired to his hotel at 10 p.m., where he took delivery of six bottles of Veronese wine to keep him oiled during nocturnal writing sessions. The resulting novel was panned by the critics, who dubbed it "Across the Canal and into the Bar" and dismissed it as a thinly veiled, alcohol-addled autobiography.

Hemingway's Venetian sojourn marked a tranquil period in a devil-may-care existence. He had survived World War I—having been badly injured by a mortar shell in Italy—and his reporting career had thrust him into the thick of the Spanish Civil War and World War II. Meanwhile, his experiences among the bullfighters of Spain, the game-hunters of the African savannah and the literati of Paris had inspired some of the greatest short stories and novels of the 20th century.

Hemingway still managed to pack in heroic antics during his stay in Venice. Regulars at Harry's Bar recall him crashing into the establishment—his face purple and his beard frozen after a day of hunting or skiing—forever the larger-than-life action hero.

How many glasses of wine does it take get the creative juices flowing? For Hemingway, a decent session at this Venetian bar followed by six bottles of Amarone just about hit the spot.

Above: The Locanda Cipriani hotel, which hosted Hemingway during his Venetian stay.
Right: Several scenes from Hemingway's novel *Across the River and Into the Trees* are set in Harry's Bar.

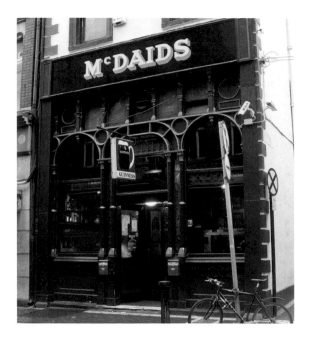

Brendan Behan Ireland

HOW TO GET THERE

The nearest airport is 11 km north of the city, and offers good bus connections to Busáras, the central bus station. McDaid's is around a 25-minute walk away: head south down O'Connoll Street, across the River Liffey and down Westmoreland Street, around Trinity College into Grafton Street, and take a right into Harry Street. While you're in Dublin, don't miss the Writers Museum on Parnell Square. Although a tad dusty, it provides an interesting introduction to the lives and work of Behan, Beckett, Joyce, Yeats, Wilde and others.
McDaid's, 3 Harry Street, Dublin 2
www.ireland-guide.com/establishment/mcdaids.4309.html
www.writersmuseum.com

Brendan Behan set out his stall out early. In 1939, aged just 16, he smuggled explosives into England for the Irish Republican Army, was caught red-handed and served 22 months in Borstal. By the end of the 1940s he had spent two further stints behind bars: four years for attempting to murder two detectives and a short stretch for violating an order forbidding him to enter England. Meanwhile, he was developing a heavy drinking habit, which fuelled bouts of violence and ill-health. He died, a chronic alcoholic, at just 41.

Amid this frenzy of self-destruction, Behan found time to turn out novels, short stories, plays and poetry in both English and Gaelic. He wrote his first play while incarcerated, and by the 1950s was addressing such topics such as the Irish struggle for independence, religion and the lot of the ordinary man with wry wit and an earthy "everyman" sensibility.

By far the best place to contemplate the writer's life is McDaid's—Behan's favourite bar and still one of the best watering holes in his home city. You'll find it in Dublin's Georgian southside—an elegant quarter that's home to Trinity College, the National Gallery, well-kept canal-sides and squares, and busy pedestrianised streets frequented by buskers and poets.

Although now firmly on the tourist trail, McDaid's remains a quintessential Irish boozer.

Formerly a Protestant meeting hall and a morgue, the pub boasts a Victorian façade, stained-glass windows and high ceilings. Inside you'll find an intimate bar, crowded with wooden tables, and walls sporting photographs of Behan and his fellow Irish literati: James Joyce, Flann O'Brien, J.P. Donleavy, Patrick Kavanagh and Liam O'Flaherty were all regulars. When not sinking pint after pint at the bar, Behan could usually be found crammed into a corner, bashing out his latest work on a battered typewriter.

To fully immerse yourself in the Behan experience, bring along a copy of his autobiographical novel *Borstal Boy*—an account of his imprisonment as a teenager—or his Gaelic play, *An Giall* (*The Hostage*)—a satirical take on Irish identity and the IRA. Both are said to contain people based on characters he met at McDaid's.

While you're there, you could test the veracity of this Behan tale with locals. Legend has it that the writer was asked to pen a strapline for Ireland's famous stout, Guinness. He was paid upfront with kegs of the black stuff, which he imbibed at an unholy pace. When Guinness chased Behan for the work, he presented them with the line "Guinness makes you drunk".

Drinker, fighter and fully paid-up member of the IRA, this Irishman's life was filled with so many wild times, it's a wonder he had time to write at all.

Left and above: McDaid's, a favourite haunt of the writer.
Right: Brendan Behan (1923–64) at work: "I am a drinker with writing problems".

"If you're paid for being crazy, then you're not crazy,
is that right?" Hunter S. Thompson (1937–2005).

HOW TO GET THERE

Puerto Rico's main airport is Luis Muñoz Marín International, located near the capital of San Juan. Take a bus or taxi to Loíza, a 25-minute drive west from the capital on the north-east coast. The town boasts an Afro-Hispanic community, having been settled by Nigerian slaves in the 17th century, and is most famous for its Fiestas Patronales—a nine-day party of salsa dancing and parades. Part of the United States since 1898, Puerto Rico is part Caribbean island, part sprawling resort. Escape the high-rise hotels and overpriced restaurants though, and you'll find unspoilt beaches, plantations and tropical forests. Don't miss the El Patio de Sam in San Juan—it's where the writer enjoyed many a local slug of rum.

www.gonzo.org | www.escape.topuertorico.com

Hunter S. Thompson Puerto Rico

Hunter S. Thompson was the archetypal fast living creative. The American's appetite for adventure, drugs and alcohol was colossal. He was jailed for robbery, spent a year on the road with the Hell's Angels—who eventually beat him up for writing about their exploits—and had a habit of scaring acquaintances witless by toting loaded guns. His hedonism fuelled a revolutionary, fast-paced, deeply autobiographical and frequently embroidered writing style, dubbed "gonzo journalism".

To understand the origins of Thompson's approach, take a trip to the town of Loíza in Puerto Rico. Then a 22-year-old budding journalist, Thompson travelled to this Caribbean island in 1960, holing up in a wooden house on the beach. It's a land of tropical forests, coconut plantations and long lazy days, and Thompson made it his home for a year. He drank, chased women and wrote for several publications, including the sports magazine *El Sportivo*, and even managed to supplement his income by modelling for Bacardi Rum adverts.

Thompson's novel *The Rum Diary* is the product of that decadent year—following the adventures of a foreign reporter and a world of belligerent bosses, corrupt officials and drunken brawls. It was eventually published in 1998 and is being made into

a film starring Johnny Depp. "I was writing about what it was like to be among vagrant journalists", Thompson commented. "Fiction is based on reality unless you're a fairy-tale artist…You have to get your knowledge of life from somewhere." The foundations of the gonzo novel were laid.

It's easy to dismiss much of Thompson's work as macho myth-making, but closer inspection reveals a desire to expose the iniquities of American life, and a healthy irreverence lacking in much modern media. He covered sport, music and politics with incisive verve, his targets ranging from crackpot foreign policy to the ailing American dream. He was a ruthless critic of George W. Bush and fiercely opposed the 2003 invasion of Iraq. In a world of spin and covert media control, Thompson's visceral rants were often closer to the truth than his critics would have us believe.

After a lifetime of chronicling his own hedonism, Thompson put a pistol to his head on February 20, 2005. According to his instructions, his ashes were shot out of a cannon amid a huge firework display. Hunter S. Thompson went out, as we always knew he would, with an almighty bang.

"I have to get paid for my vices somehow," Hunter S. Thompson famously opined, "or else it's gonna be destructive." So how did this writer turn decadence into a lucrative art form?

Thompson's *The Rum Diary*, set in Puerto Rico, contains elements of his famous gonzo style—fully developed in his most famous work, *Fear and Loathing in Las Vegas*. Thompson felt that fictional works were often closer to the truth than so-called objective journalism.
Left: Hunter S. Thompson (with pipe), Paul Semonin (with football) and Bob Bone (lighting a cigarette) at a small cement-block cabin on the beach in Puerto Rico, where Thompson and Bone were living temporarily. The photo was taken in late 1959 before Sandy (his future wife) joined Hunter there and the two moved to Loíza.

HOW TO GET THERE

London is served by four international airports, Heathrow, Gatwick, Luton and Stansted, all less than an hour by train from the city. You'll arrive at one of London's mainline stations: take the underground Piccadilly Line to Piccadilly Circus. Soho and the French House lie just a few hundred yards north of this tube stop. Soho is bordered by Shaftesbury Avenue to the south, Regent Street to the west, Oxford Street to the north and Charing Cross Road to the east. For a good evocation of the area's heyday, read Daniel Farson's book, Soho in the Fifties. The capital's Chinatown and some of its best galleries and theatres are all nearby.

Soho, London
www.ilovesoho.co.uk | www.visitlondon.com

Soho England

Dip into any pub in this lively London quarter, and the chances are you'll be standing on a spot where at least one writer or artist has crashed to the floor after hours of dedicated excess. Casanova, Francis Bacon and William Burroughs were just some of *bon vivants* who gravitated here to seduce, smoke and drink for proverbial England.

You'll find Soho in the very centre of the capital: barely half a hectare of pavement cafes, gay bars and restaurants, dotted with sex shops and the odd strip club. A recent clean-up may have closed its seedier peep-shows, and many of its legendary landlords are now pulling pints in the sky, but the area still possesses a certain louche edginess. Prostitutes still tout *sotto voce* from doorways, and it's surprisingly easy to find yourself in a subterranean drinking den at 5 a.m.

To understand Soho, we need to go back to the 17th century. Then open farmland, the area was appropriated by Henry VIII as a royal park—the hunting cry of "soho!" christening the district. After the Great Fire of 1666, the fields gave way to much-needed housing. Although initially built for the wealthy, the area quickly became a refuge for Huguenots fleeing persecution in France under Louis XIV's reign. Greeks, Russians, Italians, Poles and Germans followed, generating an unfettered mélange of cultures and trades.

By the mid-1800s, the combination of low rents, bawdy taverns, brothels and theatres made Soho a magnet for intellectuals and artists. Residents included W. A. Mozart, Percy Shelley, Karl Marx, Canaletto, William Blake and John Constable. For many, Soho's cultural zenith came between the 1930s and the 1960s, when it was supposedly impossible to enjoy a quiet pint without bumping into T. S. Eliot, George Orwell, Virginia Woolf, George Bernard Shaw or a dribbling Dylan Thomas.

The best way to explore Soho is to embrace that fine British institution—the pub crawl. Start at the French House on Dean Street, which hosted French Resistance meetings during the World War II. The perpetually packed bar can still muster the high-calibre banter of Bacon's day. From here, head north to the Dog and Duck on Bateman Street, a Victorian establishment frequented by Orwell and, more recently, Madonna. Call into Greek Street's Pillars of Hercules to raise a glass to former patron Charles Dickens, and then re-group up the road at the Coach and Horses, the hangout of journalist and dedicated vodka drinker Jeffrey Bernard. Through a creeping fug of inebriation, you should start to understand the true spirit of Soho, just before you set your sights on the next bar.

From louche low-lifers to wealthy media moguls, outrageous artists to gin-soaked journalists: this London enclave is an enduring draw for creatives off the leash and on the lash.

Left and above: High rents have put Soho out of reach for struggling artists and writers today, but it retains its boho credibility thanks to pubs such as The Pillars of Hercules and The Coach and Horses.
Right: Soho in the 1950s: The Windmill Theatre and Italian café life.

The US's Burning Man festival attracts thousands of creative revellers (left). The Guatemalan village of Todos Santos marks the Day of the Dead with daredevil horse races (right).

DEBAUCHERY FOR BEGINNERS

Beirut

Already partied at BO18—Beirut's famous bunker club that opens up to the night sky? Then try the city's hottest new venue: the Starco Building's Music Hall is a hybrid club and live-band space, hosting top DJs plus musicians from Cuba, Spain, Russia and elsewhere.
Entry: €26/$33.
www.destinationlebanon.com

Thailand

It may look like the interior of the world's most fashionable space rocket, but this establishment specialises in serving quality cuisine while you stay horizontal. Bangkok's Bed Supperclub combines restaurant, bar, art gallery and performance space, hosting acts ranging from graffiti artists to top DJs. The menu is quality Med-meets-Asian.
From €25/$32 for dinner.
www.bedsupperclub.com

Iceland

Got buckets of money and celebrity ambitions? Head for Kaffibarinn in Reykjavik—part-owned by Blur's Damon Albarn—and blow a month's wages on some cocktails. Cult waster flick *101 Reykjavik* was filmed here, and don't turn up before 2 a.m. or you'll be on your own—the Icelandic party scene kicks off late.
www.icelandairwaves.com

Ukraine

Let Rimbaud take you by the hand into a land of velvet and some rather impressive chandeliers. Part restaurant, part lounge, Kiev's Decadence House is decked out like a late 19th-century Parisian saloon, offering hookah pipes, acres of sofas and a brace of libraries for the bookish. And once you've had your fill of black caviar you can even have a go at the pole dancing. Cuisine is Italian/Japanese.
www.carteblanche.com.ua/en/rest/decadence

United States

OK, so it may not be able to guarantee a naked Bianca Jagger on a white horse every night, but this reincarnated Studio 54 does promise bungee jumpers, acrobats, top DJs and cheesy 1970s' moves. Its home is the MGM Grand in Las Vegas, so slap on some glitter and get down.
Entry: €8/$10 for men, women free.
www.studio54lv.com

Hungary

Famous for its lively arty crowd, this is a city bar as it should be: packed with old-skool furniture, retro cartoons and healthy levels of irreverence until the early hours. You'll find the Szoda bar in the Erzsebetvaros district, within a siphon's squirt of some of Budapest's best architecture and museums.
www.szoda.com

MEDIUM-PACED EXCESS

Morocco

Even Miss Marple couldn't fail to score a carrot-sized reefer in this country. For natural highs, head for the Rif Mountain town of Chefchaouen—a hub of hashish production. It's one the most chilled corners of the country, proving that cannabis thwarts even criminal urges. Remember, although the drug is smoked in Morocco, it is officially illegal. Lay your floating head at the medina's Casa Hassan.
From €59/$72 per night.
www.casahassan.com

Germany

More than six million visitors imbibe a heady mix of music, beer and partying at this annual beer festival, held in Munich. Highlights of Oktoberfest, which confusingly starts in mid-September, include parades, the tapping of the keg ceremony, Bavarian canon salutes and—for those with cast-iron stomachs—a funfair.
Beer from €6.65/$8 a litre.
www.oktoberfest.de

India

Forget Pancake Day: the Goa Carnival is the only real way to prepare for Lent. With its origins in the debauchery of ancient Rome, this February free-for-all comprises three solid days of drinking and dancing, while parades and bands blast their way through the streets. If you have the funds, try the upmarket Pousada Tauma.
From €215/$269 per night (peak season).
www.pousada-tauma.com

Cuba

Time to take to the streets and throw ludicrous shapes in the most outlandish outfit you can find. Santiago's Fiesta del Fuego lasts for a full week in July and features carnival parades, Caribbean tunes and gallons of omnipresent Havana rum. Free.
www.cubatravel.cu

Ireland

It's a simple formula: you go on a pub crawl of Dublin's finest watering holes, while a brace of musicians provides the entertainment. Traditional Irish music is interspersed with anecdotes, resulting in a good few hours of quality craic.
€12/$15.
www.discoverdublin.ie/musicalpubcrawl.html

Brazil

A few pints at your local, or a two-million-strong bash on a beach in South America? It's a tricky one, but Rio de Janeiro's "Réveillon" New Year's Eve knees-up might just have the edge. Head for Copacabana Beach and stand well back as 25 tonnes of fireworks go up in smoke. Try the Insider's Guide to Rio de Janeiro for accommodation.
www.riodejaneiroguide.com/newyears

THIS IS HARDCORE
United States

For 8 days in late summer, some 30,000 people throw themselves into a frenzy of self-expression on an ancient Nevada lakebed. The result is the Burning Man festival: radical installation art, loony costumes, loud tunes and an almighty inferno finale. The event is commerce-free, so you need to bring all supplies and be prepared for harsh desert conditions. From €196/$250.
www.burningman.com

Europe & Africa

Leave the millionaires to their boys' toys in the Dakar Rally, and go hell-for-leather from Hungary to Mali in West Africa in this low-budget alternative. The Budapest to Bamako Rally runs 8,000 hard kilometres through eight countries and takes in the Sahara Desert. The cash-strapped can even hitch their way round. From €300/$365 per person.
www.budapestbamako.org/en

Spain

Billed as Spain's most outrageous party, Sitges Carnival sees a quarter of a million gay and straight partygoers pack this Catalan coastal town. Standby for outrageous drag acts, a grand parade and as many local dishes as you can get your puckered lips around. And to recover, chill out on one of the good beaches nearby.
Free.
www.sitges.com/carnaval

France

Every tried canyoning? Chamonix-based Rush Adventures cater for adrenaline junkies keen on sampling this new sport—which essentially involves throwing yourself down a river and then abseiling, jumping and scrambling your way out. Ice climbing, paragliding, rock climbing and scaling Mont Blanc are also on offer. Accommodation from €36/$44 per night; canyoning €65/$79 per session.
www.rushadventures.co.uk

Guatemala

Here, November 1 celebrations combine vast quantities of alcohol with horse racing, often with fatal consequences. The male population of Todos Santos, a village high up in the mountains, marks the Day of the Dead by drinking itself into oblivion and then cantering madly along a muddy track. Tourists with a death wish can take part.
Free.
www.gonomad.com/destinations/0012/koch_todos_santos.html

Scotland

Described by the BBC as "not so much a game…more a civil war", the Kirkwall Ba' is a mass free-for-all football match with no rules. Every Christmas Day and New Year's Day, the male residents of Kirkwall divide into two teams, each vying to heft a cork-filled leather ball to their opponents' end of town. Tempers fray, but injuries are surprisingly rare.
www.orkneyjar.com/tradition/bagame

Jamaica & Worldwide

Singles weekends, full-on naturism, "Ms No Swimsuit" breaks—a Hedonism holiday revives the art of Bacchanalian excess. Either that or you'll spend a week being ogled by a builder from Scunthorpe—the risk is yours to take. Over 18s only. From €815/$1,037 per person for seven nights
www.hedonism-resorts.info

Philippines

Need to kick the city dust off your shoes? Take to the saddle of a Honda XLR20 and explore the tropical rainforests, beaches, active volcanoes and mountain tracks of the Philippines on a 14-day motorcycling adventure. White-water canoeing and scuba diving will mop up any excess adrenaline. H-C Travel also runs bike treks throughout the world.
Rider: €1,799/$2,174; passenger: €975/$1,178
www.hctravel.com

Kim Ki-duk (1960–).

Kim Ki-duk   South Korea

HOW TO GET THERE

The nearest major airport is Seoul's Incheon International, situated 52 km west of the city. The most straightforward route involves picking up a coach direct to Juwangsan (5 hrs). From there take a bus to Jjeon (20 mins) situated 5 km from the reservoir. You'll do the last stretch by taxi and on foot. Jusan Reservoir, Juwangsan National Park, North Kyungsang www.korea.net | www.sonyclassics.com/spring www.npa.or.kr/chuwang/english/html/culturalo1.html

This tale should hearten all amateur filmmakers. Kim Ki-Duk dropped out of school at 17, laboured in factories, and served in the South Korean Army. Then, after a two-year stint in France—where he touted his paintings along the streets—he tried his hand at writing and directing films.

With no formal training, Kim conjured up a string of outsiders to explore unsettling themes of suicide, betrayal and violence. Although initially poorly received in his native South Korea, Kim's work has since been heaped with accolades—including the 2000 Sundance Film Festival's World Cinema Award. Screenings at film festivals in Moscow, Berlin, Venice and Helsinki have put the director on the crest of South Korea's "New Wave" of cinema.

Kim's methods are unorthodox: he eschews scripts, preferring to capture sparse dialogue as it develops on location. He often shoots scenes in real time, but favours giant temporal leaps too, often spanning decades. Location is critical—he uses small, isolated worlds to play out universal, almost mythic, themes.

For an insight into Kim's eye for setting, visit South Korea's Juwangsan National Park. It's a hiker's paradise: treks run through spectacular gorges and forests via Buddhist temples, waterfalls, ice caves and snow-capped mountains. Kim fought for six months for permission to shoot *Spring, Summer, Autumn, Winter…And Spring* on the park's Jusan Reservoir—an artificial lake built in 1721.

The tale was filmed entirely on the lake, with most of the action taking place on a wooden Buddhist temple, floating in its centre. The film follows the vicissitudes of a monk and his apprentice over a lifetime, the seasons marking five stages of man: the ebullience of youth, the lust of first love, the rage of betrayal, contrition and, ultimately, renewal. Buddhist themes—from universal respect to the dangers of attachment—are woven into the narrative. It's a beautiful, utterly absorbing work, and as good an illumination of Buddhism as you're likely to find over 103 minutes.

You'll find the park offers a host of natural wonders that vary, as you would expect, according to the time of year. In spring you should walk the Jubang valley, which will be carpeted with wild red azaleas. In summer the forests are at their most verdant, while in autumn the trees are a riot of russet and amber. In winter, the park is transformed into a rugged land of snow and ice. And the Jusan Reservoir—fringed with weeping willows and reflecting the towering Taebaek Mountain Range—is a fine spot to escape the hurly-burly of modern life, whatever the season.

Frustrated by the shallowness and stresses of modern life? The Jusan Reservoir, located deep into the mountains of South Korea, could provide exactly the Zen space you need.

Right and following double page: *Spring, Summer, Autumn, Winter…And Spring* was filmed on South Korea's Jusan Reservoir, which draws visitors throughout all four seasons.

Above and right, above: The Ganges runs from the Himalayas through Rishikesh.

HOW TO GET THERE

The nearest regional airport is Jolly Grant, 24 km away. Rishikesh is situated 238 km north of Delhi. To get there by train head for Haridwar, a town 24 km south of the town, and take a bus, taxi or auto-rickshaw from there. Alternatively there is a direct bus from Delhi (6 hours). Rishikesh comprises five distinct settlements so chose your accommodation carefully. Lakshman Jhula is one of the quietest places to stay. The Maharishi Mahesh Yogi's Ashram has now closed down, but there are several other ashrams nearby that you can stay in, in addition to numerous hotels. Courses in yoga, meditation and Ayurvedic studies are on offer, alongside more frenetic and seasonal pursuits such as river rafting and trekking. Be wary of the river—the Ganges' currents are particularly strong and many visitors have lost their lives here.

Lakshman Jhula, Rishikesh, Uttaranchal
www.beatles.com | www.rishikesh.org | www.thebeatlesinindia.com

The Beatles India

Over a few days in early 1968, a series of battered taxis rattled through the dust into a small town in the Himalayan foothills. Out stepped some of decade's biggest stars including Mia Farrow—fresh from her split from Frank Sinatra—Mike Love of the Beach Boys and Donovan. By far the most famous, however, were four young men from Liverpool. Their aim? To study transcendental meditation under the Maharishi Mahesh Yogi.

The Beatles' India trip was extremely timely. Their recent psychedelic studio album *Sergeant Pepper's Lonely Hearts Club Band* had left the band creatively frazzled. A media frenzy and the clamour of their fans showed no sign of abating. Transcendental mediation, which claimed to stimulate reserves of creativity and energy and induce a state of inner calm, looked a good escape route from the drugs, wealth and fame. The band threw themselves into ashram life, with John and George in particular immersing themselves in sessions lasting several hours.

The group gained from the experience, although enchantment with ashram life varied from member to member. Ringo, who had arrived with a suitcase full of baked beans to avoid the local cuisine, was the first to leave after just ten days. Even-keeled Paul put in a respectable five weeks, while George and John

managed two months, before a confrontation between Lennon and the Yogi prompted a return to England. Eventually the band grew suspicious of the Yogi's money-making drive, as he was soon cashing in on his association with the group by branding himself as guru to the Beatles.

Listen to the band's White Album and you'll see how the trip had a major effect on the band's output. Bereft of studio gizmos, full orchestras and powerful hallucinogenics, Lennon and McCartney turned to acoustic-based compositions and simple, heartfelt narrative-based structures. The band penned more than forty songs in just eight weeks, going on to create a work that spanned reggae, vaudeville, psychedelic sound collage, country, rock'n'roll and even proto-heavy metal.

When you visit, head for the suspension bridge that spans a cobalt twist of the Ganges at Lakshman Jhula—one of five villages that make up Rishikesh. According to Hindu mythology, the penance of the sage Raibhya Rishi was rewarded with an appearance of God on this spot. Looking down onto the river spilling onto the plains of India, it's easy to see why this settlement endures as one of the most restorative places in the world, guru or no guru.

The spiritual beauty of Rishikesh draws hordes of pilgrims and mediation enthusiasts every year. Where better for the world's most famous pop group to recuperate?

Right: The Beatles spent several weeks in 1968 at the Maharishi Mahesh Yogi's Ashram in Rishikesh.

Sergio Leone (1929–89). His Spaghetti Westerns were initially labelled violent crowd-pleasers by critics, but are now hailed as being among the greatest films of the 20th century.

Sergio Leone Spain

HOW TO GET THERE

The nearest airport is Almería, situated around 24 km from Oasys. The best way to get to Oasys is to hire a car: take the N-340 north out of Almería, following signs to Murcia and Tabernas. You'll find the set 7 km south of Tabernas. While you're in the area, make sure you visit two other film locations: the nearby Texas Hollywood was used to film parts of *The Good, the Bad, and the Ugly*, while *Once Upon a Time in the West* was filmed at a third set, Western Leone, situated 2 km outside Tabernas. Texas Hollywood is thought by some to be the most authentic of the three sets and offers accommodation in wooden cabins and horses treks.

Oasys, Texas Hollywood, Western Leone, Tabernas, Almería
www.hvsl.es/lei/hojas/leio0002.htm | www.fistful-of-leone.com

The tension is almost unbearable. Two gunslingers stand a hundred paces apart, their faces weather-beaten and expressionless. The sun beats down, the saloon doors creak in the breeze and the town holds its breath. Silence reigns. Then, in a flicker, one man draws his gun and fires. His opponent drops to his knees, and his life seeps away into the dust.

It's a classic cowboy duel, and it happens at least once a day in Oasys (formerly Mini-Hollywood)—the set built for the Sergio Leone's Spaghetti Westerns of the mid-1960s. Now a theme park, actors enact dramatic shoot-outs and raids among the town's saloon and assorted stores, while visitors play can play extras if the mood takes them.

You'll find the town in Europe's only desert, Tabernas: a dry sierra of ochre outcrops, canyons and rugged mountains, baked dry under the sun of southern Spain. Despite its commercialism and hammy actors, you should just embrace the cowboy fantasy when you visit: there can be fewer better spots to ponder the achievements of Italians Sergio Leone and Ennio Morricone.

In the 1950s, Westerns were largely US-made, sanitised affairs with cheesy songs around the campfire and clearly defined good guys and bad guys. Director Sergio Leone sought to create an entirely different world; a gritty land inhabited by battle-worn, inscrutable and nameless vagabonds, stripped down to their primal states by life on the harsh plains. A minor actor by the name of Clint Eastwood took the central role, while Leone's old school friend, composer Ennio Morricone, provided the scores: sparse arrangements replete with jackal cries, whip cracks, Mexican trumpets and dramatic choral chants.

Leone's timing was good. By the early 1960s, the film industry was smarting from flops such as 1963's *Cleopatra*, and expensive epics had fallen out fashion. Leone's stylised, low-budget Westerns were a gift. His first effort, *A Fistful of Dollars*, was a re-make of the Japanese film, *Yojimbo*—the story of a samurai arriving in a remote town and manipulating two rival gangs. Leone transplanted the narrative into a Wild West setting, and produced a huge box-office hit in 1964. For *A Few Dollars More* and *The Good, The Bad, And the Ugly* followed, completing the Dollars trilogy.

In just four years, Leone and Morricone had entirely re-made the Western: haunting musical motifs stood in the place of dialogue, while atmosphere and characterisation were generated by achingly long scenes, wide-angle shots and close-ups. The "man with no name" had arrived: cool, instinctive, violent and utterly mesmerising.

The story was Japanese, the director Italian, the setting Spanish and the cast hailed from all over the world. No wonder these Westerns looked like nothing cinema-goers had ever seen before.

Above: Clint Eastwood (1930–) as The Man with No Name in *For a Few Dollars More* (1965).
Right and following double page: Leone's westerns were filmed at three sets in the Tabernas Desert.

"We slept in peasant beds… Fleas did jumping exercises on the coverlet… We drank quantities of hard likker and gallons of Lapte Batute buttermilk for re-hydration." Lee Miller (1907–77) on her trip, which also featured tyre blow-outs, a car crash and a massage from a bear.

Lee Miller Romania

HOW TO GET THERE

Romania's major airport is Otopeni, situated around 20 km from Bucharest. Make sure you spend some time in the cosmopolitan capital—once dubbed "Paris of the East"— the Roman town of Sibiu, the capital of Transylvania and the medieval city of Brasov. Beyond the cities you'll still find good skiing, mountain biking and hiking territory. The UK abode of Lee Miller and Roland Penrose is also open to visitors by appointment (tel: + 44 (0)1825 872 691). The Sussex farmhouse remains largely unchanged since Miller's death, and contains a good collection of work by the photographer, Penrose, Man Ray and others. Miller's son, Antony Penrose, runs guided tours. www.leemiller.co.uk | www.romaniatravel.com

It's a far cry from genteel photo shoots with Fred Astaire or Charlie Chaplin. Here we have images of tough rural harvests, primitive wooden carts, dancing bears and children playing mountain horns. The photographs capture everyday life in Eastern Europe just before the outbreak of World War II. They also mark a watershed moment in the life of Lee Miller.

Born in 1907 in New York state, Miller led one of the most extraordinary lives of modern times. By her mid-twenties she had been a Vogue cover girl, muse to the surrealist movement in Paris, a lover of Man Ray and the owner of a successful New York photographic studio. But by her late thirties, Miller had reinvented herself as a fearless photojournalist, capturing bomb-torn London, Liberation Day in Paris, the Normandy beaches after D-Day and the horrors of Nazi concentration camps.

These Romanian pictures, taken in 1938, mark a critical change for Miller—the former studio-based photographer was now an adventurous chronicler of life in foreign climes. In 1934 she had married Egyptian millionaire Aziz Eloui Bey and moved to Cairo. But after four years of married life, she grew bored of bridge parties and photographing ancient monuments, and embarked on a tour of Greece and Romania with the surrealist artist Roland Penrose. The couple travelled to remote Romanian villages, accompanied by ethno-musicologist Harry Brauner, capturing rituals and traditions soon to be swept away by the war. A keen journalistic sensibility was born.

By 1940 Miller had split from Bey and was living with Penrose in London. Calling upon her newfound reportage skills, she threw herself into the heat of the Blitz, contributing shots of the splintered capital to British Vogue. Her appetite for war duly whetted, she became a war correspondent with the US Army in 1942.

Visit Romania today, and you'll still find scenes redolent of Miller's 1938 trip. The horse and cart is still used, and the countryside ranks among the most spectacular in Eastern Europe, featuring ancient monasteries, wetland reserves and the Carpathian Mountains. In particular, the Dracula territory of Transylvania retains much of its rustic simplicity.

In 1945 and 1946, Miller was back in Eastern Europe, by now a battle-hardened war correspondent intent on exposing the harsh realities of post-war life. She travelled through Austria, Hungary and Romania to file disturbing images of death camps and children dying in hospital through a lack of drugs. These pre- and post-war studies reveal Miller's greatest talent: the ability to record both gut-wrenching conflict and everyday peacetime with equal honesty.

Lee Miller was the darling of the surrealist movement, and a feted photographer of some of the 20th century's greatest icons. So what prompted her transformation into a gutsy war correspondent?

Below: Lena Constante, artist and wife of Harry Brauner, seen here with her puppet of Hitler at the close of World War II.

Right: Little girl with an alpenhorn in the Apuseni mountains.

Right: Ox in a cart.
"She broke out of the studio in Egypt and into documentary in
Romania." Antony Penrose, director of the Lee Miller Archive, on his
mother. Miller returned to Romania in 1945 to discover that most of
the gypsy families she had photographed in 1938 (below) had been
massacred.

Jürgen Hohmuth (1960–) has travelled the world to take photographs with his seven-metre-long "blimp" airship.

Jürgen Hohmuth   Germany

HOW TO GET THERE

Berlin is served by three airports—Tegel, Schönefeld and Tempelhof—all connected to the city by good transport links. You're likely to spend much of your time in Auguststrasse, in the historic centre of Mitte, and Prenzlauer Berg: both districts are home to a high concentration of galleries. The international Art Forum Berlin fair runs in the autumn, while the biennale is held in the spring (dates vary). Don't miss Tiergarten's Hauptbahnhof, Berlin's spectacular new railway station. Classic tours take in the Brandenburg Gate—built in 1791 and symbolising peace—the Holocaust Memorial, and a stretch of the Berlin Wall, re-erected in 2004. Berlin also boasts good nightlife, parks and rivers. And if you fancy joining the city's artistic community, you can still find relatively cheap studios and accommodation.

www.smb.museum | www.berlinfo.com
www.berlin-tourist-information.de/index.en.php
www.zeitort.de

If any city can claim to be a thriving cultural hub it's Berlin. When the Wall fell in 1989, young artists and galleries flooded into the crumbling Auguststrasse district to seed a vibrant creative community. Since 1996, more than 25 museums have opened or been renovated, taking the city's enviable total to more than 170. Meanwhile, Berlin's art biennale and heavyweight architectural commissions such as Daniel Libeskind's Jewish Museum have put the city firmly on the cognoscenti radar. The city manages to balance historic and cutting-edge attractions, so you're as likely to stumble across an avant-garde digital installation as a stunning Prussian façade or a Caravaggio.

Chronicling this collision of old and new required some innovative thinking, and Jürgen Hohmuth developed the perfect device. The landscape and architecture photographer felt frustrated by shooting from aeroplanes and helicopters—the distances were too great—and so in 1999 turned to mini-airships for a more intimate view. Seven years and three balloons later, Hohmuth perfected a helium-filled tethered "blimp", enabling him to photograph subjects from vantage points ranging between ten and one hundred metres off the ground. The photographer doesn't ascend with his seven-metre-long airship, but

controls the camera from the ground via a video link.

"The practice of taking photographs from balloons is at least 150 years old", commented Hohmuth. "But modern technology makes it a new thing. I can take high definition stills and even video in every direction. It's a very free form of photography."

You could happily plan your tour of Berlin around Hohmuth's aerial escapades. Start with the Unesco World Heritage Site of Museumsinsel (Museum Island), located between the Kupfergraben and the River Spree. Built between 1824 and 1930 as a "sanctuary of art and science", the area's five museums were almost entirely destroyed in World War II, and are now being restored and modernised. Collections run from classical antiquities to 19th-century masterpieces. You should also take in the Reichstag—the German parliament building spectacularly redesigned by Norman Foster—and the bohemian district of Prenzlauer Berg, still popular with artists and a young international set despite rising rents.

Hohmuth has filled several books with his aerial photographs, capturing subjects as diverse as Berlin's Holocaust monument and labyrinths and mazes across Europe. Forthcoming projects will take him to the White Sea in Russia, India and Morocco.

His first balloon came a cropper on a peach tree near Dresden; the second met a sticky end on an antenna. But Jürgen Hohmuth persevered, and his "mark III" floating camera captured stunning "angel's eye" views of Berlin's cultural gems.

Reunification of East and West Germany in 1990 led to a cultural boom in Berlin, particularly in the historic central Mitte district of former East Germany.
Right, top: Norman Foster's Reichstag.
Right, bottom: Potsdamer Platz.
Following double page, clockwise from top left: Unter den Linden; the Victory Column; the Brandenburg Gate; Daniel Libeskind's Jewish Museum.

HOW TO GET THERE

The nearest airport is Lugano-Agno, situated 42 km away. You can also fly to Zurich or Milan, both around 3 hours away by train. There are good connections from all three airports to Locarno train station. For the final leg, take an "eco taxi" direct to Monte Verità (tel. 0800 321 321) or pick up the 31 bus to Ascona (15 mins) and walk from there (20 mins). Don't miss Ascona's galleries, including the Museo Comunale d'Arte Moderna, plus the botanical park on the Isole di Brissago, 4 km south. And for a good insight into the history of Monte Verità, read Mara Folini's *The Mountain of Truth*, published by the Swiss Society of Art History.

Monte Verità, Via Collina, CH-6612 Ascona
www.monteverita.org | www.switzerland.isyours.com
www.csf.ethz.ch/about/location/trainMV

Modern-day Monte Verità continues to explore art and science through seminars and conventions.

Monte Verità Switzerland

If you had visited this Swiss enclave a century ago, you would have left your inhibitions, and quite possibly your clothes, at the door. During its heyday, Monte Verità attracted anarchists, pacifists, artists, vegetarians, philosophers, dancers and nudists in droves. Their aim? To escape the mores of modern society, forge a new, unadulterated way of life, and push the boundaries of human expression.

Monte Verità—literally "Mountain of Truth"—was founded in 1900 by Henri Oedenkoven, the son of a wealthy industrialist, and the pianist and feminist author Ida Hofmann. They established the retreat on a wooded hillside above Ascona, a fishing hamlet on Lake Maggiore's northern shore, and couldn't have chosen a better spot. Soft hills, palms and citrus fruit trees abound thanks to a mild sub-tropical microclimate, while its telluric magnetic currents are thought to stimulate creative thought.

The colony's first inhabitants built a clutch of wooden huts and started to explore "Reform of Life" principles. They lived off the land, threw themselves into hearty exercise, staged theatre and dance shows, and practised heliotherapy—the art of treating illness through direct exposure to sunlight.

By 1913, the establishment of the School of Natural and Expressive Dance switched the focus to frolicking naked in the open air. When World War I broke out, the colony evolved again: artists, intellectuals and pacifists flocked here from all over Europe. Over three decades, visitors included Hermann Hesse, Paul Klee, Isadora Duncan and James Joyce. But by the 1940s, the counter-culture party was over. Wealthy holidaymakers moved in.

Visit today though, and you'll find that progressive ideas are still enthusiastically pursued, albeit by a more sober, clothed crowd. Now comprising a smart Bauhaus hotel, conference centre, restaurant and museum, Monte Verità continues to explore spirituality, science and art through seminars and conferences. Initially re-opened for serious academic debate, it now also hosts regular concerts, plays, exhibitions and gastronomic evenings for locals and visitors.

So what of the legacy of those radical days? Dadaism was born here, while Hesse drew on his lakeside experiences for much of his fiction. The colony also played in a role in the development of the Bauhaus, psychoanalysis and the radical performance collective, Cabaret Voltaire, as well as the UK's Bloomsbury group. In the end, the utopian enclave that attracted suspicion and schoolboy sniggering, inspired some of the most influential ideas of the 20th century.

This colony rejected modern science and industry in favour of a bucolic life. But what did a counterculture built on home-grown vegetables, naked dancing and free love actually achieve?

Right: Monte Verità was established as a utopian community. Residents staged theatre and dance shows, grew their own vegetables and lived a healthy outdoor life.

Above and right: Pablo Picasso (1881–1973) working in his Vallauris studio. He first became interested in ceramics in his twenties but left it until his sixties to take up the art form full-time.

Pablo Picasso France

HOW TO GET THERE

The nearest airport is Nice, situated 24 km east along the coast. Take the bus—or better still, the scenic Nice-Tende-Cuneo train route—along the coast to Golfe-Juan, situated 4 km west of Cannes. Take a bus or a taxi the 1.2 km inland to Vallauris, where you'll find a plethora of galleries, markets, craft shops and good restaurants. You'll find some of Picasso's ceramics at Galerie Madoura, situated in Rue Georges et Suzanne Ramié. Don't miss Picasso's L'Homme au mouton sculpture in Place Paul Ismard. The Biennale Internationale de la Ceramique runs from July to November. Golfe-Juan is a family-friendly resort boasting two good beaches.

Musée national Picasso, La Guerre et La Paix, Place de La liberation, 06220 Vallauris

www.musee-picasso-vallauris.fr | www.picasso.fr

One summer's day in 1946, Pablo Picasso stopped off at an exhibition of local pottery in Vallauris, a sleepy town on the Côte d'Azur. Intrigued by the work, he sought out a studio and proceeded to throw a few small pieces. Within two years, Picasso had upped sticks from Paris and settled permanently in the south of France. In an intense 15-month burst of creativity, Picasso produced some two thousand ceramic works. In his mid-sixties, the 20th-century's greatest artist had reinvented himself once more.

Picasso chose the right spot to pursue the art form. The area had been known for its fine clay soil since the 16th century, and remains famous for tiles and decorative pieces to this day. And at two kilometres inland from Golfe-Juan, the town offered the tranquility of the Mediterranean, without the Riviera bustle of nearby Cannes or Grasse.

Those first Vallauris works were hugely varied, comprising decorated plates, female figures, vases, jugs and animals such as bulls and fauns. By the early 1950s Picasso was producing more graceful, ambitious pieces: vases adorned with veiled and nude women, Arcadian dancers and musicians, dishes displaying bull-fighting scenes viewed from above and fragments bearing figures and profiles. Exhibitions throughout Europe

followed, and the art world celebrated a new era in ceramic art.

The relocation also prompted a final—and rare—period of stability in Picasso's tangled romantic life. By the time he moved to the South of France he had been married twice, conducted countless affairs and had fathered four children with three different women. He moved to the village with his latest partner, Françoise Gilot, but in 1952 met Jacqueline Roque at Madoura Pottery—the studio where he created those first works. Gilot left him a year later, and by 1955 he and Roque were living in a villa overlooking the Bay of Cannes. They married in 1961, when Picasso was 79, and she became his last love.

Picasso's legacy has put Vallauris on the tourist trail, but despite huge visitor numbers it still manages to retain its charm. You'll find some of those extraordinary ceramics at the Musée Picasso La Guerre et La Paix. The neighbouring Château de Vallauris also showcases modern ceramics from the region.

If you feel like picking up your own Picasso work, take care to do your homework before you write your cheque. "Originals" were designed and painted by the artist, and can sell for up to $350,000. His "editions" meanwhile, although designed by him, were decorated by his assistants and can sell for as little as $350.

Imagine, just for a moment, that you're the world's most famous living artist. Having broken boundaries in painting and sculpture countless times, you're now seeking a new challenge. For Picasso, the answer lay in the South of France.

Above: A typical town house in Vallauris.

Above: Robert Johnson (1911–38) was particularly careful to keep his playing style secret and refused to elaborate on his techniques.

Robert Johnson United States

HOW TO GET THERE

The nearest airport is in Memphis, situated 112 km north of Clarksdale, although you'll probably arrive by one of America's two favourite forms of transport—the Greyhound bus or the car. Don't miss Morgan Freeman's club, Ground Zero, and the world's largest collection of Johnson-related materials at the Greenwood Blues Heritage Museum & Gallery in Greenwood, situated 90 km south of the town. Clarksdale also hosts the Sunflower River Blues and Gospel Festival in August. Be aware there are two other putative crossroads: the south end of Rosedale at the intersection of Highway 8 and Highway 1, and where Jonestown Road crosses Highway 61. Mississippi, although badly battered by Hurricane Katrina in 2005, is still a major draw for music fans, and those who want to enjoy the quiet backwaters of its undulating landscape and historic towns. Highways 61 and 49, Clarksdale, Mississippi www.visitmississippi.org | www.gcvb.com | www.deltahaze.com/30/rj.html www.threedeuces.net

One cool night in October 1930, a cotton worker strode to the crossroads of Highways 61 and 49 just outside Clarksdale in the Deep South. At midnight, under the light of a bright full moon, he recited a mantra to summon the devil and made a pact—his soul in exchange for a sublime musical gift. The encounter re-tuned his guitar and left the young man with an otherworldly blues sound, but condemned him to an early death at just 27 years old.

In truth, it was probably personal tragedy rather than a nocturnal assignation with Lucifer that transformed Johnson from lacklustre guitarist into legendary bluesman. But it's such a spellbinding tale—a compelling amalgam of Faustian pact, African folklore and good old-fashioned propaganda—that to question its veracity is almost to miss the point. The blues feeds off dark tales of loss, witchcraft and encounters with the spirit world, and this story captures the genre's essence perfectly.

In April 1930, Johnson's newborn baby and 16-year-old wife died in childbirth. The same year, he met bluesman and preacher Son House, famous for a raw, emotional style. Johnson, until then a sharecropper and guitarist of modest talents, threw himself into music. He adopted an itinerant lifestyle, leaving his home in Robinsonville to play juke joints and levee camps throughout the Deep South, learning from other blues guitarists as he travelled. Johnson returned a changed man, a charismatic performer with a closely guarded playing style that astounded audiences.

Whatever you believe, there's no denying the guitarist's extraordinary talent. Johnson went on to play to adulating crowds as far afield as Chicago, Detroit and New York; and Elvis Presley, Led Zeppelin's Jimmy Page and Eric Clapton all subsequently cited his influence. For proof, track down his 1936 and 1937 recording sessions—for which he received paltry cash payments and no royalties—and marvel at the supernatural melancholia of *Terraplane Blues*, *Hellhound On My Trail* and *Cross Road Blues*.

Clarksdale may have lost much of the rustic simplicity—Johnson's crossroads is now a busy intersection—but you can still track down the haunting blues sounds that he pioneered. Try the town's Blues Alley district for sessions, while the Delta Blues Museum houses a good collection of memorabilia.

Johnson's fate was actually sealed by his two other loves—drink and women. During a performance near Greenwood in 1938 he took a slug of whisky, thought to have been laced with strychnine by a jealous husband. The bluesman was dead within three weeks.

Woke up this morning in the mood for the blues? Head for this town on the Mississippi Delta—the birthplace of John Lee Hooker, Johnny B. Moore and the world famous legend of the crossroads.

Above: Robert Johnson's famous crossroads at the intersection of Highways 61 and 49 outside Clarksdale. Just eleven 78 rpm records were released during his lifetime, but his sound has been far-reaching with the likes of Eric Clapton and Led Zeppelin among his fans. Right: The spirit of the blues lives on.

Following double page: The cotton plantations of the Deep South.

John Hinde (1916–98).

HOW TO GET THERE

Butlins' three resorts are all in England: Minehead, Skegness and Bognor Regis. All three are well served by public transport and are within easy access of the UK's major airports. Bognor Regis is home to the Shoreline Hotel—an upmarket establishment boasting smart family rooms and penthouse suites. For a glimpse of those early days, check out the original 1930s' chalet, preserved for posterity next to the hotel. Butlins still prides itself on offering affordable family holidays, and accommodates 1.3 million guests a year. Bognor Regis is one of the sunniest places in England, and boasts a historic coastline and good beaches. You'll find a collection of Hinde's Butlins photographs in the book, *Our True Intent is All For Your Delight* (published by Chris Boot).

Butlins, Minehead, Skegness, Bognor Regis
www.butlins.com | www.chrisboot.com
www.sussexbythesea.com

John Hinde — England

Flick through picture postcards of the British Isles from the early 20th century, and you'll find a plethora of static and largely uninspiring monochrome scenes. But skip to the decades after World War II, and you'll be treated to a riot of technicolour and vigorous activity: super-saturated hues depict glowing individuals at work and at play. Pioneering the revolution was Englishman John Hinde.

Starting out in London in the early 1940s, Hinde was one of the first photographers to contribute colour images to magazines. An assignment for the book *British Circus Life* led to a disastrous spell running his own circus, but in the 1950s he hit upon the idea of printing colour postcards. Hinde recruited a coterie of German photographers, and proceeded to build one of the most successful postcard publishers in the world.

Hinde was a canny operator: he capitalized on Ireland's tourism boom by delivering bucolic scenes of caravans, Irish dancers, donkeys and simple country folk. Keen to portray a tourist-friendly idyll, he concealed unsightly elements using judiciously placed rhododendron branches—usually purloined from a nearby garden. He also garnered major commissions, including one from the entrepreneur Billy Butlin.

Butlin opened his first holiday camp in Skegness, on the east coast, in 1936. The concept was revolutionary: a place where workers could enjoy bracing sea air, ballroom dancing and light-hearted entertainment such as "glamorous granny" competitions—all for a week's wages. The formula proved a huge success: by 1961 there were nine camps, and by the 1970s more than a million people a year were enjoying a Butlins holiday. Who better to capture the spirit of the times than Hinde?

Hinde's Butlins postcards, produced in the late 1960s and early 1970s, are some of his studio's best work. Pioneering depth-of-field and colour techniques produced hyper-real images of themed bars, ballrooms, pools and restaurants, all produced in large-format ektachromes. While Hinde took a supervisory role, the shoots were executed by his colleagues Elmar Ludwig, Edmund Nägele and David Noble.

The advent of the foreign package holiday in the 1970s severely dented Butlins' fortunes, and a series of sell-offs has left just three resorts. That said, the 21st-century has seen a much-needed injection of cash and ideas: smart apartments and a state-of-the-art hotel have replaced chalets, while entertainment now features live bands and world-class circus acts. Meanwhile the famous Redcoat entertainers—a Butlins' institution since its inception—still provide a vibrant dash of colour.

As the austerity World War II lifted, thousands headed for the seaside to enjoy a Butlins holiday. Photographer John Hinde helped replace leaden grey with revitalising colour.

Above: Butlins' new Shoreline Hotel in Bognor Regis.
Right: Bognor Regis is a popular family-holiday resort, even today.

Scenes from Butlins Bognor Regis.
Clockwise from top left: The Blinking Owl Bar by David Noble;
Lounge adjoining indoor heated pool by Edmund Nägele;
The Pig and Whistle Bar by David Noble.

Yang Yong (1975–).

Yang Yong   China

HOW TO GET THERE

The nearest airport is Shenzhen International, connected to the city centre (32 km) by regular shuttle buses. The city is well served by public transport, with numerous buses and sightseeing tours. If you take a taxi, insist that the driver uses the meter. The best way to reach Overseas Chinese Town (OCT) is by taxi (around $10 from the airport). While you are there you can always call in at Yang Yong's studio (email: yangyong1975@yahoo.com.cn). OCT Contemporary Art Terminal, Overseas Chinese Town, Shenzhen www.o-cat.net | www.sz.gov.cn/english/city/default.htm

If you want to see China's booming economy at its most unfettered, take a trip to this south-coast city. Once a small fishing village and stop-off port on the Silk Road, Shenzhen was designated a "special economic zone" by leader Deng Xiaoping in his sweeping 1970s' reforms. In just three decades years, paddy fields have given way to shopping arcades, theme parks, ports and thriving industrial zones, while its population has grown from thirty thousand to more than eight million.

This breakneck growth has spawned a new breed of thrusting entrepreneur, and is now even redefining what it means to be Chinese. It's also produced a new breed of uncensored artist: among them, cutting-edge photographer Yang Yong. Born in Sichuan province in south-west China, Yang originally trained as an oil painter, but moved to Shenzhen and started to record the urban explosion using video. He then turned to photography to chronicle daily life in the city, taking particular interest in the millions of residents migrating from throughout China.

Yang's works are unashamedly honest depictions of the minutiae of life amid rampant consumerism. In a 2006 London exhibition, *Between Past and Future*, he depicted the urban boom through super-saturated, dynamic skylines. Meanwhile, his solo exhibition *Women are Beautiful Always and Forever* comprised a series of portraits of Shenzhen prostitutes. Neither voyeuristic, sensationalist, nor pitying, they attempted to record city life as he saw it. "This is one reality of China", Yang commented. "I do not care whether or not a woman is a prostitute. I am just trying to show how people really live."

When you visit Shenzhen, you'll find it easy to find the artist's raw materials beyond the heavily promoted folk villages, safari reserves and amusement parks. For the best bars and live music, head for the grittier district of Futian or the entertainment quarter of Shekou. For good contemporary art, try the He Xiangning museum and the Overseas Chinese Art Terminal (OCAT), both situated in Overseas Chinese Town (OCT) on Shenzhen Bay.

Before long, you'll see the truth in a local saying: "You think you're brave until you go to Manchuria, you think you're well read until you reach Beijing, and you think you're rich until you set foot in Shenzhen".

The boom town of Shenzhen, found on the Pearl River Delta, is one of the fastest-growing cities in China. Photographer Yang Yong has chronicled its growth, warts and all.

Right, top: Yang Yong, *The Cruel Diary of Youth—Dusk of the Gods No. 56,* 2000.
Right, bottom: Yang Yong, *Xiaoyin Alone No. 12,* 2002.
Following double page: Yang Yong, *The Cruel Diary of Youth No. 90,* 2003.

A host of energy-healing and detox treatments are on offer at Finland's Mairela Cottage (far left) and Lanzarote's Holistic Holidays (right), while Shining Minds offers self-realisation workshops in the UK and India (far right). Cross-Cultural Solutions (near left) runs volunteer projects for communities in Africa, Asia, Latin America and Eastern Europe.

QUICK HITS
Spain

Get back to nature with a stay in a traditional yurt, set amid cork trees and olive groves in the mountains of Andalucía. The Hoopoe Yurt Hotel is also the perfect spot for brushing up on your riding and pottery skills, while yoga, reiki and massages are also on offer. There's a pool and mini-yurts for the kids too.
€85/$79 per night.
www.yurthotel.com

United Kingdom

From arts and heritage to the environment and youth mentoring, do-it.org.uk puts you in touch with a vast range of volunteering opportunities in your area. Commit yourself for between just a few hours and several days a month. Provides good advice and links for overseas opportunities too.
Free.
www.do-it.org.uk

Greece

A guru and dogma-free zone, this Greek island retreat gives visitors the opportunity to rethink their lives and determine what really matters. Skyros activities include yoga and life-coaching, while more adventurous types can windsurf, sail, dance and paint, or enjoy offbeat cabaret at a sister centre on the other side of the island.
From €640/$896 per week.
www.skyros.co.uk

Worldwide

The pen truly is mightier than the sword. International Pen promotes freedom of expression through a community of professional writers, editors and translators, in particular campaigning for the rights of those persecuted for expressing their views. There are 141 centres, which also run events and literary prizes.
www.internationalpen.org.uk

United Kingdom/India

Need to put some fire in your belly? Shining Minds runs self-realisation workshops and coaching at retreats in Devon, England and in Kerala, India. Depending on your needs, sessions can help you achieve your life goals, improve performance at work, cultivate a healthy work/life balance, or simply restore vitality.
From €431/$525 per break.
www.shiningminds.co.uk

Finland

Jaded, fatigued or plain fed up? Mairela Cottage offers a plethora of energy-healing treatments including reiki, meditation, detoxification and lifestyle advice. The tranquil setting might provide tonic enough: you'll be on the edge of a lake surrounded by forest, and in prime fishing and walking territory. Treatments complement conventional medicine.
From €365/$439 per week.
www.mairela.com

Lanzarote, Canary Islands

Relax and rejuvenate with a host of holistic therapies—including reflexology, reiki, shiatsu, detox massage and yoga—at this island retreat. Holistic Holidays' villa boasts its own pool and botanical garden, while Lanzarote's beaches and volcanic beauty are within easy reach.
From €348/$422 for a long weekend.
www.hoho.co.uk

India

This Indian retreat attracts those looking to meditate, rest or swim in upmarket environs. Situated in Pune, Osho's 40-acre campus features an Olympic-sized swimming pool, marble pathways and a forest of tropical foliage. Classes include yoga, tai chi, chi kung and poi dance. Try and bag a room in the minimalist guesthouse.
From €43/$52 per night.
www.osho.com

MEDIUM-TERM
Worldwide

You don't need to be a teenager with a chin stud to travel the world. Gap Year for Grown Ups helps over-30s plan a globe-trotting break and take part in volunteer programmes or skill-building adventures lasting days or months. Options include big-game monitoring in Africa, house-building in Sri Lanka and maintaining orang-utan trails in Borneo.
From €721/$874 for four weeks.
www.gapyearforgrownups.co.uk

Worldwide

Keen on volunteering abroad but can't spare a year or two out? Cross-Cultural Solutions enables you to spend between one and 12 weeks working on vital community projects, ranging from orphanages and childcare centres to schools and health clinics. You'll work alongside local people and the emphasis is on experiencing the culture of the country. Projects run in Africa, Asia, Latin America and Eastern Europe.
From approx. €1326/$1,595 for a week.
www.crossculturalsolutions.org

Italy

Forget evening classes under leaden skies; the only real way to learn Italian is to live in the country. Umbria's University for Foreigners is one of the best places to immerse yourself in Italian culture, offering affordable tuition fees and low living costs. You'll be in the historic city of Perugia, a short hop from Tuscany and Rome. Courses run from one to six months.
Fees from €400/$486.
www.unistrapg.it

Africa

Live, work and travel in some of the most stunning and remote regions of Madagascar with Azafady—an award-winning charity devoted to alleviating poverty, improving livelihoods and protecting the environment. Its ten-week volunteer programme is very hands-on, so you could be doing anything from planting trees and installing wells to conducting lemur surveys in the forest. From €2,867/$3,488.
www.madagascar.co.uk

Worldwide

This ski-resort job finder will see you mastering fakeys within weeks. Choose from a huge range of seasonal employment, from reps and bar staff to nannies, maintenance chefs and *plongeurs*. The pay isn't great, but with free food and accommodation, lift pass and ski gear, becoming king of the mountains doesn't come cheaper.
Free.
www.natives.co.uk

Worldwide

Fancy dipping your toe into another culture but don't want to splash out on expensive hotels? HomeExchange.com enables you to swap your house or apartment with some 10,000 members based in more than 90 countries worldwide. Stays can be anything between days and months, while you've a choice of mountains, beaches, big cities, and much more.
Membership: €47/$60 for a year.
www.homeexchange.com

France

This Buddhist monastery and retreat helps visitors weave "mindfulness" into everyday life, hosting stays of up to three months. Located 85 km east of Bordeaux, activities at Plum Village go beyond meditation and recitation to talks, walking and communal cooking. From €270/$330 per week.
www.plumvillage.org

India

Feed the spirit and mind at this Zen center, found in the Perumal Hills of South India. You can spend weeks in silent meditation, working towards enlightenment and "freedom from attachment". Bodhi Zendo boasts an idyllic garden and panoramic views of mountains and valleys. Classes are free. €4/$5 per day.
www.bodhizendo.org

RADICAL CHANGE
France & Worldwide

Desperate times call for desperate measures. Although no longer a refuge for renegades on the run, joining the French Foreign Legion still allows you to adopt a new identity. You enlist in France, but could serve in any of the country's overseas territories or conflicts involving the mother country.
www.legion-recrute.com/en

Europe & Australasia

Fancy moving lock, stock and barrel abroad? Just Landed advises on living, studying and working in Europe, Australia, and New Zealand, offering guides on everything from visas and work permits to rental advice, healthcare, and job hunting.
www.justlanded.com

New Zealand

New Zealand offers a rare combination of natural beauty, work/life balance and go-head attitude. Relocations International advises on everything from shipping your belongs to temporary accommodation, buying a house, education, tax, immigration law and even baby-sitting.
www.relocate.co.nz

Worldwide

Seeking full-on immersion in a new culture rather than a quick sample? Go Abroad.com lists more than 100,000 opportunities to study, live, work and volunteer overseas. A global searchable database helps you pinpoint your options, and you'll find good eco-adventures in the Himalayas, Costa Rica and beyond.
www.goabroad.com

Author's Acknowledgements

Creating this book has involved high drama, jubilation and several buffeting storms. Firstly, my thanks go to my publisher, Philippa Hurd, who has kept the boat afloat with excellent navigation skills and some spirited pumping of the bilges. My picture researcher, Natalie Buchholz, also deserves several medals for her perseverance, as does Kieran Wyatt for his subbing skills and Caroline Jones for her meticulous fact-checking. Stu Smith and his design team have somehow found a few more stops to pull out, resulting in a design that's nothing short of a triumph. My greatest thanks go to my wife Sarah, who has endured many months of living with an unshaven, bleary-eyed writer. I would like to dedicate this book to our son, Monty, born this year. Many helpful individuals around the world have also taken the time to help me, for which I am extremely grateful.

Thanks to:
Jyoti Adhikari, Anthony Allen, Tau Apollonius, Laura Arias, Elizabeth Bähr, Peter Barratt, Chris Bland, Eva Bodinet, David Bratman, Julia Brooke, David Buckland, Josic Cadoret, Claudia Lafranchi Cattaneo, Alfredo Cefalo, Tim Chester-Williams, Rebecca Chetley, Rose Cholmondeley, Carole Chrétiennot, Steve Clarke, Liz Clayfield, Guiseppe Colella, Corrine Cordero, Michael Cross, Michael Davies, Candice Davey, Rajina Day, Patrick Deese, Agustín Dorado, Cass Douglas, Laurent Echaubard, Hugh Epstein, Anna Faithfull, Isobel Falk, Lucio Fava del Piano, Emanuela Ferrero, Bruce Foerster, Stuart Forster, Randy Gardner, Claudio Giorgione, Antony Gormley, LeRoy Grannis, Andie Grace, Michael Green, Dr Chris Grogan, Georg Guðni, Niv Hachlili, Sigal Hachlili, Helen Harrison, Peet van Heerden, Bill Hinchberger, Joanne Hindle, Meera Hindocha, Guy Hinton, Jürgen Hohmuth, Frater Hrumachis, Auður Gná Ingvarsdóttir, Pete Johnson, Antony Jones, Bernard Khoury, Kate Kraczon, Berit von Kurnatowsk, Ed Kushins, Joanne Looby, Adam Latham, Sarah Latham, Françoise Lemieux, Christian Marclay, Phil Martin, Kevin McCullagh, Zac McDuffle, Martin McIver, Carla Merriman, Sebastian Michael, Kate Millar, Mary Morzinski, Simon Murie, Paula Nirschel, Christopher North, Dr Bernfried Nugel, Catherine Oakes, Alice O'Hanlon, Chutima Ongsanthia, Julio Osorio, Joel Oury, Heather Owen, Lesley Penniston, Maria Perez, Judith Pillinger, Jennifer Porcella, Lauren Potters, Andrew J. Poulton, Shirley Purves, Anne Ridsdale Mott, Amanda Robinson, Paul Saltzman, Sujit Sarkar, Dr Felizitas Schreier, Andreas Schwab, Lisa Sheard, Dr Allan Simmons, Claudia Spahr, Paul Spiring, Sandra Squires, Zoltan Sugar, Michael Tavani, Alexis Thornely, Susie Thornhill, Rihs Tobi, Jonathan Toubin, Sam Trenerry, Lady Susana Walton, Martin Wardrop, Emma Watson, Maurice Watson, Jo Wheeler, Kathryn Whitehead, Brandon Wick, Mark Wilby, Lucja Wisniewska, Greg Wolf, Rachael Wood, Harald Vatne, Iren Vatne, Alessandra Vinciguerra, Kolbrún H. Víðisdóttir, Ariella Yedgar, Yang Yong.

Many thanks to the following organisations for assisting with the book: Aboriginal Art Galerie Bähr, Aboriginal Art Online, The Britten–Pears Library, Byronmania, Butlins, Café de Flore, Cape Farewell, Centre for Aldous Huxley Studies, The Chopin Society, Discover the World, European Space Agency, Gustav Klimt Memorial Society, Initiative To Educate Afghan Women, Jean-Michel Cousteau Fiji Islands Resort, La Mortella, Martin Randall Travel, London Sherlock Holmes Society, Modern Art Oxford, Monte Verità, Mornings in Mexico, Museo Nazionale della Scienza e della Tecnologia Leonardo da Vinci, Natural History Museum, Ocean Futures, Patriarch Thelemic Gnostic Church of Alexandria, Papunya Tula Artists Pty Ltd, Paula Cooper Gallery, Particle Physics and Astronomy Research Council, The Photographers' Gallery, Pollock-Krasner House and Study Center, The Regent Experience, Sogndal & Luster Tourist Office, SwimTrek Swimming Adventure Holidays.

Publisher's Acknowledgements

The Publisher is grateful to the following for their help in the preparation of this book:

Elisabeth Bähr, Aboriginal Art Galerie Bähr, (with thanks for advice on text and pictures); Christine Barberi, Gallery Director, and Ilse Schache, Goedhuis Contemporary; Chris Boot and Bruno Ceschel; Bonifacio Brass, Locanda Cipriani; Rose Cholmondeley, Chopin Society of the UK; Carole Chrétiennot, Café de Flore; Dr. Nicholas Clark, Curator for Reader Services, The Britten–Pears Library; Jean-Michel Cousteau Fiji Islands Resort; Tom Ordway, Jean-Michel Cousteau's Ocean Futures Society; Elmgreen & Dragset; ENIT, München; Arwen Fitch, Press Officer, Tate St Ives; Esther Quiroga, Galerie Klosterfelde, Berlin; Randy Gardner; LeRoy Grannis; Harry's Bar; Jule Hartung, Tartan Films; Victoria Hermosa, OASYS, Parque Temático del Desierto de Tabernas, Almería; Damien Hirst; Jürgen Hohmuth, (www.zeitort.de); Robyn Katkhuda; Kunstverein Springhornhof, Neuenkirchen; Bob and Kandi Kimbrough, The Delta Blues Museum, Clarksdale Mississippi; Isabel King; Ralf Knochner, (www.nanaziesche.com; www.umdiewelt.de); Jana Juni, Lee Sung-Won, Yong-Yeol, Kim Chang-Hwan, Kim Gwan-Hyeon, Hwang Man-Bok, Korea National Park Service; Claudia Lafranchi, Monte Verità; Steve LaVere (with thanks for advice); Alistair Leach, Artificial Eye Film Company Ltd.; Madeline Leahu, Waterways Department, Environment Agency; Sandra Leitte; Philippa Lewis, Edifice Picture Library; Bobby Marcuson; Maysam Makhmalbaf; Guy Moreton; Michael Nedo, Wittgenstein Archive; Corinne Occhipinti, Maison du Tourisme de Vallauris Golfe-Juan; Julio Osorio; Amanda Parmer, Paula Cooper Gallery; Doyle Piland, White Sands Missile Range Museum; Gabrielle Redmond; Sylvie Rigoulet, Comité Régional de Tourisme de Normandie; Janette Scott, Cape Farewell; Julia Sheppard; Bernd Sinterhauf; Smithsonian National Museum of African Art; Conor Sweeney (www.Dublinpubs.ie); SwimTrek (www.swimtrek.com); Café Tortoni; Tourismusverband Ferienregion Attersee; Mark Vernon-Jones; Anthony Wallis, Aboriginal Artists Agency; John Warburton-Lee; Deborah West, Tourism Officer, Sussex by the Sea (Arun District Council); Mark Wilby, The Owl House; Yang Yong.

Picture Credits

All reasonable efforts have been made to obtain copyright permission for information quoted and images reproduced in this book. If we have committed an oversight, we will be pleased to rectify it in a subsequent edition.

Cover, top to bottom: Mark Hannaford/John Warburton-Lee Photography; © LeRoy Grannis; © Presented by Korea National Park Service © Magnificent view of autumn scene by Hwang Man-Bok; © Courtesy: Art Production Fund, New York/Ballroom Marfa, Marfa/the artists © Photo James Evans

Back flap photo: Stu Smith

p. 8 www.budapestbamako.org

INSPIRATION

12 Amar Grover/John Warburton-Lee Photography
13 © SV-Bilderdienst: 90100/KPA/HIP
14–15 Mark Hannaford/John Warburton-Lee Photography
16 top left: © SV-Bilderdienst: Scherl
bottom right: Mark Hannaford/John Warburton-Lee Photography
17 Mark Hannaford/John Warburton-Lee Photography
18–19 Mark Hannaford/John Warburton-Lee Photography
20 top left: Photo: Steven Gross. Courtesy Paula Cooper Gallery, New York
bottom right: Christian Marclay, *Sound Sheet*, 1991. Clear flexidiscs & white thread 156 1/2 x 99 inches (391.2 x 251.5 cm). Courtesy Paula Cooper Gallery, New York.
21 Christian Marclay, *Video Quartet*, 2002. Four-channel DVD projection, with sound, running time: 14 minutes. Each screen: 8 x 10 feet; overall installation: 8 x 40 feet. Courtesy Paula Cooper Gallery, New York
22–25 © Julio Osorio
26–27 © Georg Guðni
28–29 Julian Love/John Warburton-Lee Photography
30 Edifice/Kim Sayer
31 Edifice/Gillian Darley
32–35 © Café Tortoni, Buenos Aires
36 © SV-Bilderdienst: 90100/KPA/HIP
37 Purchase of Ivory, French Congo [now Republic of Congo]. Photograph by Robert Visser, c. 1882–1894, postcard collotype. Publisher unknown, c. 1900. Postmarked October 24, 1911. EEPA Postcard Collection CF 16 7. Eliot Elisofon Photographic Archives. National Museum of African Art, Smithsonian Institution
38–39 John Warburton-Lee/John Warburton-Lee Photography
40 top left © Ealing / The Kobal Collection
bottom right: Jonathan Lee
41–43 Malcolm MacGregor/John Warburton-Lee Photography
44–45 © estate of the artist licensed by Aboriginal Artists Agency 2006/Photo: Bernd Sinterhauf
46–47 © Aboriginal Art Galerie Bähr/Photos: Lindsay Frost
48–51 © Cape Farewell and the Artists

CREATION

55–57 Courtesy of the Artist and Jay Jopling/White Cube, London
Antony Gormley, *Inside Australia*, 2002/2003
Cast alloy of iron, molybdenum, iridium, vanadium and titanium. 51 elements based on 51 inhabitants of Menzies, Western Australia. Commission for 50th Perth International Arts Festival, Western Australia, 2003
58–61 Mark Wilby, Owl House Foundation
62 top: © Paul Gauguin. Photograph by Boutet de Monvel, c. 1891
64 Paul Gauguin, *Little Black Pigs*, 1891. 35 3/4 x 28 3/8 in. (91 x 72 cm). Museum of Art Budapest
65 Paul Gauguin, *Where Do We Come From? What Are We? Where Are We Going?*, 1897. 54 3/4 x 147 5/8 in. (139 x 375 cm). Museum of Fine Arts, Boston, Tompkins Collection. © Photo: Giraudon, Paris
66 © Courtesy: Art Production Fund, New York; Ballroom Marfa, Marfa; the artists
67 © Courtesy: Art Production Fund, New York; Ballroom Marfa, Marfa; the artists/photo: Lizette Kabré
68–69 © Courtesy: Art Production Fund, New York; Ballroom Marfa, Marfa; the artists © Eise Frederiksen
70 © Bowness, Hepworth Estate
71 Julian Love/John Warburton-Lee Photography
72 left: © Bowness, the Hepworth Estate. Photo: Marcus Leith and Andrew Dunckley © Tate 2004
right: © Bowness, the Hepworth Estate. Photo: Bob Berry
73 © Bowness, the Hepworth Estate. Photo: Bob Berry
74 Courtesy The Wittgenstein Archive/Michael Nedo
75 Photo: Guy Moreton
78 © Baback Haschemi, haschemi ® edition cologne
79 © Guy Bouchet
80 top: © Chopin Society of the UK
bottom: Sandra Leitte
81 © Chopin Society of the UK
82 Photo: Hans Wild. Courtesy of The Britten-Pears Library, Aldeburgh
83 top: Photo: Nigel Luckhurst. Courtesy of The Britten-Pears Library, Aldeburgh
bottom: Courtesy of The Britten-Pears Library, Aldeburgh
84–85 © 2003 Aldeburgh Productions. Photo: Paul Morris
86 Photo: Cecil Beaton

192 INDEX OF NAMES